1964

1964

THE GREATEST YEAR IN THE HISTORY OF JAPAN

HOW THE TOKYO OLYMPICS
SYMBOLIZED JAPAN'S MIRACULOUS
RISE FROM THE ASHES

ROY TOMIZAWA

LIONCREST
PUBLISHING

1964 – THE GREATEST YEAR IN THE HISTORY OF JAPAN
*How the Tokyo Olympics Symbolized Japan's
Miraculous Rise from the Ashes*

ISBN 978-1-5445-0371-4 *Hardcover*

978-1-5445-0369-1 *Paperback*

978-1-5445-0370-7 *Ebook*

Author photo by Kevin Ing.

This book is dedicated to my family lineage: my grandfather and grandmother, Kiyoshi and Fumi, who moved from Japan to America at the turn of the twentieth century, my parents, Thomas and Sayoko, and my son, Sean Kiyoshi.

CONTENTS

PREFACE

On the opening day of the 1964 Tokyo Olympics, October 10, 1964, I turned one.

My father, Thomas Tomizawa, was in Tokyo working with the NBC News crew that broadcasted the XVIII Tokyo Olympiad to homes in the United States. I still treasure the various souvenirs he brought back from Asia's first Olympiad.

My father, Thomas Tomizawa (standing left), with Rafer Johnson (seated) on NBC News team, courtesy of Roy Tomizawa

As a teenager, I proudly wore my 1980 NBC Moscow Olympic T-shirt, likely the only kid in Queens, New York, to have one.

I have been a fan of the Olympics for a long time.

When I moved to Japan for a third time in 2014, a year after Tokyo was awarded the right to host the 2020 Games, I went to the Japanese bookstore, Kinokuniya, in search of a book in English on the 1964 Tokyo Olympics. None were in print.

So, I decided to write that book.

A former journalist myself, I began my research in late 2014, copying all that I could in the National Diet Library.

At the beginning of January 2015, I interviewed American gymnast, Makoto Sakamoto, the first of over seventy Olympians from sixteen different nations who participated in those 1964 Summer Games. Many of the quotes in this book are directly from those Olympians.

On May 1, 2015, I launched my blog, The Olympians (https://theolympians.co/). For over a thousand straight days, I obsessively published an original blog post on anything related to the 1964 Tokyo Olympics, the Olympics, Japan, and sport in general.

The blog, in essence, became my first draft for this book.

The book, in essence, became my weekend meditation, and an expression of my deep appreciation for Japan, and a fascination for Japan's biggest postwar moment.

INTRODUCTION

THE HAPPY GAMES IN THE
EYE OF THE STORM

In 1964, Japan was getting ready for the biggest party in the world—the Summer Olympics.

Olympic officials were working around the clock to manage Japan's most complex peacetime event ever. Japanese athletes were steeling themselves to compete against world-class performers. Engineers and construction firms were rushing to complete massive plans for highways and railways, stadiums and hotels. Government officials and teachers were educating the public on how to best present themselves to the tens of thousands of foreigners that would pour into Japan. Police were taking pickpockets off the streets and ensuring bars in Tokyo were complying with directives to close down early. The Japan Self-Defense Forces were preparing for their supporting roles in various events such as sailing and rowing.

In fact, every man, woman, and child in Japan was getting ready to welcome the world to their country, many believing it was their civic duty to ensure that foreigners who came to town were not deprived of any necessity or assistance. A resident of Shibuya remembers as a child that the ward office instructed all Japanese to convert the toilets in their homes (essentially holes in the ground) to flush toilets, on the off chance that a foreigner might visit them. So the man's mother took out a loan and made the change.

His father, who worked for the railways, began to study English at his own expense on the slight possibility that he might have to guide a foreigner to the right place. Everyone, it seemed, was catching Olympic fever, even his neighbor:

> In the summer of 1964, we had less rain. When I sprinkled water on the street in front of my house, a neighbor got angry with me, saying, "Save water for the foreigners," as if he regarded me as an unpatriotic man.[1]

---

1   Satoshi Shimizu, "Rebuilding the Japanese Nation at the 1964 Tokyo Olympics: The Torch Relay in Okinawa and Tokyo," in *The Olympics in East Asia: Nationalism, Regionalism, and Globalism on the Center Stage of World Sports* (New Haven: Yale University, 2011) 42.

The Japanese were determined to show the world that they could host the Summer Olympic Games, the first in Asia, and regain the world's trust after the upheaval of the Second World War. Nothing could distract them from this mission. Not even the clamor of geopolitical conflict and social change taking place in and around the two weeks of the Tokyo Olympics, October 10 to 24.

And there were lots of distractions.

- Only two months before the start of the Olympics, on August 4, a battle between US and North Vietnamese military boats was said to have taken place in the Gulf of Tonkin, with a second attack said to have taken place two days later. In consequence, the US Congress passed a resolution, which in effect justified the deployment of US conventional forces in Vietnam to "defend against communist aggression."
- On September 24, only ten months removed from the assassination of American President John F. Kennedy, the Warren Commission, headed by Supreme Court Chief Justice, Earl Warren, presented its 888-page report to President Lyndon B. Johnson, with the hopes of defusing the growing rumors of widespread conspiracy.
- On October 3, only a week prior to the start of the Tokyo Olympics, fifty-seven East Berliners nervously

walked through a tunnel dug under the Berlin Wall, to escape to freedom in West Berlin.

- On the third day of the 1964 Tokyo Olympics, October 12, the Soviets took the world by surprise—launching the first three-man spaceship in history into orbit. The *Voskhod* circled the earth fifteen times, raising the rhetoric on which superpower was winning the space race.

- On October 14, the fifth day of the Tokyo Olympiad, one of the most powerful men in the world, USSR first secretary, Nikita Khrushchev, was deposed from power by his own Communist Party, news that stunned the world. That same day, it was announced that Martin Luther King Jr. had won the Nobel Peace Prize.

- Two days later, the People's Republic of China detonated an atomic test bomb, sparking fears of atomic fallout over Japan, the only nation to have suffered nuclear attack.

It is incredible to think that so much of global significance happened that autumn of 1964, particularly during those two weeks of the Tokyo Olympiad. And yet, it seems, relatively few were tuned in to the raucous geopolitical noise of the time. When informed afterwards, many of the participating athletes were surprised to hear so much was happening in the world around them. In retrospect, they realized they were deep in their cocoon of concentration.

But so were the people of Japan. Only nineteen years after the physical and moral devastation of defeat at the end of World War II, after the humiliation of foreign rule into the early 1950s, Japan's attention was wholly focused on hosting an Olympics that would stand out in the annals of the event.

It is of course hyperbole to call any year the greatest year in a country's history, as is the case in this book's title. But one can argue that the XVIII Olympiad held in Tokyo, Japan, in October 1964, has become a symbol of the immense collective joy of the time, a cathartic release from the psychological purgatory of defeat in the Pacific War, subjugation by the enemy, and the painstaking recovery from destitution and despair.

Never was the nation more aligned, never was the nation prouder than in 1964—rising from the rubble to embark on the greatest Asian economic miracle of the twentieth century. The only thought most Japanese had in October 1964 was to convince the world that Japan was peaceful, friendly, productive, innovative, and modern—that they belonged to the global community as much as any other nation.

It is perhaps a measure of their success that despite all the surrounding turmoil, the Games they produced came to be known as the "Happy" Olympics.

CHAPTER 1

A FEELING OF DOOM

A DUTCH JUDOKA DEFEATS A JAPANESE AT HIS OWN GAME

THE DUTCH GIANT

It was Friday, October 23, 1964, the penultimate day of competition.

The Nippon Budokan was charged with excitement. Paul Maruyama of the United States judo team watched from the side as two giants of judo stepped up on the tatami-matted platform to face off in the finals of the Open Weight Division: Anton Geesink of Holland and Akio Kaminaga of Japan.

Judo was debuting at the Olympics, the only event native to Japan, and the Japanese had already taken gold in the first three weight classes over the previous three days. Maruyama understood that this was no ordinary match, that to sweep the judo championships in all four weight classes would set off celebrations across Japan and bring back feelings of pride that had been crushed at the end of World War II, a mere nineteen years prior.

"It was definitely an electric atmosphere," said Maruyama. "The Budokan was packed. The Crown Prince and Princess were present. But there was also a sense of resignation in the air. The spectators could see for themselves: Geesink was two meters tall and weighed 120 kilos, this big foreign guy, while Kaminaga was 1.8 meters tall and only 102 kilos."

In fact, Geesink had already shocked the judo world in 1961 by becoming the first non-Japanese to win the World Championships, defeating the Japanese champion Koji Sone. So while the Japanese in the Budokan were hoping Kaminaga would exceed expectations, hope was all they had.

Japanese novelist Tsuneo Tomita was in the Budokan that day. He saw Geesink and Kaminaga go up against one another in a preliminary round and felt that Kaminaga had lost before the match had even begun. "Geesink stood tall," he wrote, "raising both hands high in the air, readying himself for the battle, total confidence in his expression. On the other hand, Kaminaga's face was pale, and his entire body rigid. This does not look good, I thought with a gulp."[2]

Geesink then handled Kaminaga quite easily in that preliminary match.

What could be done? If Kaminaga was to face Geesink again in the medal round, a likely scenario, could he find a weakness in Geesink's formidable technique? Maruyama's teammate, exchange student Ben Nighthorse Campbell, was also a member of Kaminaga's team at Meiji University, a judo powerhouse in Japan at the time. According to Campbell, they gathered together behind locked doors to come up with ways to take Geesink down. Kaminaga then engaged in practice bouts with fellow Meiji judoka, who mimicked Geesink's style and technique, looking for that nugget of insight that would give Kaminaga a fighting chance.

During the course of the day's tournament, both men progressed through qualifying matches. Kaminaga won his bouts, but Geesink dominated in his. Tomita described

2   Tokyo Shimbun, October 22, 1964; in Tokyo Olympic—*Bungakusha ni Yoru Tokyo Gorin Zenkiroku* (Kodansha, 2015), 166.

Geesink's matches as akin to a "sole black belt tossing around a bunch of white belt novices."

Judo purists in Japan at the time believed that height and weight were less important than balance, technique, and attitude, which is why judo competitions in Japan at that time never segregated judoka into weight classes. But weight and size can make a significant difference if all other factors are equal. "In those days there was still an attitude that skill could prevail over size and weight," said Campbell, who would go on to become a two-term US Senator for Colorado. "Over time judo has changed. Size matters."

The Japanese saw themselves as smaller and weaker when compared to the West. They saw the face-off between Geesink and Kaminaga as a reminder of the Pacific War, when the bigger, stronger Americans with their bigger, stronger military weaponry ended the war with authority.

And the Japanese public still remembered Douglas MacArthur, the conquering American general who ruled over Japan from 1945 to 1951. Often seen with sunglasses and a pipe, the tall man was a towering presence who commanded respect and fear even as he earned genuine gratitude for the benevolent aspects of his tenure.

As the head of the Allied Powers in Japan, MacArthur got badly needed food and medicine to people across the country from the start. He leveled the local playing field with his economic policies and actions, in particular by purchasing land (by fiat) from the small number of large landowners and re-selling them to the tenant farmers who worked the land. And he engineered a peaceful transition from foreign rule to Japanese government.

But quite suddenly, on April 11, 1951, President Harry Truman ordered MacArthur home, ending his command of the United Nations forces in Korea, including his command over occupied Japan. Nearly a month later, at the end of a series of Congressional hearings, and after many complimentary words about the Japanese and their resilience, he made an unexpected comment that struck a nerve in the Japanese psyche.

According to historian John Dower, in his book, *Embracing Defeat: Japan in the Wake of World War II*, MacArthur compared Germany to Japan, arguing that Germany had no excuse for being the aggressor in Europe, but that Japan was a different case and that we needed to give the Japanese the benefit of the doubt despite their actions in World War II. He went on to say:

> If the Anglo-Saxon was, say, forty-five years of age in his development, in the sciences, the arts, divinity, culture,

the Germans were quite as mature. The Japanese, however, in spite of their antiquity measured by time, were in a very tuitionary condition. Measured by the standards of modern civilization, [Japan] would be like a boy of twelve as compared with [the Anglo-Saxon] development of forty-five years.[3]

At the time, that comment was a bracing slap that no doubt added motivation to Japanese efforts at recovery. By 1964 that recovery had progressed so far that Japan was able to put on an Olympiad unparalleled for its efficiency, hospitality, and technological precision, laying its claim to equal stature in the international community with the Western powers. But as the Japanese watched Geesink get ready to grapple with Kaminaga in front of the defeated emperor's eldest son, some may have recalled MacArthur's remark, or yielded to the foreboding that the larger Westerner would inevitably prove superior.

The referee motioned for the commencement of the match. Maruyama saw the intimidation start early. "Geesink was a big guy, but when he raised his arms high, he'd look huge. I think he did it so that his sleeves would slide down his arms and provide less area for his opponent to grab. But I think his opponents thought that it just made this big guy look bigger."

---

3   John Dower, *Embracing Defeat: Japan in the Wake of World War II* (New York: Norton, 2000), ebook location 9950.

"Of course, you can't compare the ravages of war to the outcome of a judo match," he went on to say, "but to many looking on there had to have been echoes of that awful, empty feeling that pervaded the country after its defeat in 1945."

For at the end of the war, only nineteen years prior, Japanese were indeed in desperate straits, both in Japan as well as its former colonies across the Sea of Japan.

Paul Maruyama knows exactly how desperate those times were. He was there.

"WHERE'S PAUL?"

"I was five years old, and I was on a train in Manchuria with my three brothers and my parents," Maruyama recalled. "With a few other kids on the train, we paraded up and down the aisles without a care in the world. There were a lot of bigger men sitting in the train car with us, and they would pick us up, and we would play with their mustaches and touch their weapons. They were Soviet soldiers, and I'm sure my parents were very nervous. But we just played and played."

The Maruyamas were on the run, seeking a safe haven in a city in China called Dalian. It was autumn, 1945. Japan had already surrendered to the US and the allied powers on August 15, 1945, and the Soviet Union had hastily declared war on Japan and overrun the imperial empire in Manchuria. Soviet soldiers were routinely ousting Japanese from their homes, taking possessions from them on the streets, and forcibly putting them to work to break down the Japanese industrial infrastructure so that machinery and scrap metal could be sent back to the Soviet Union.

Even worse, Japanese women were harassed or raped, while Japanese men were sent to work camps in Siberia. The estimated 1.7 million Japanese pioneers, bureaucrats, and civilians (not including the thousands of Japanese Imperial soldiers and their dependents) who moved to Manchuria in the 1930s and 1940s to start new lives were left to fend for their very lives when the Pacific War ended.

Paul Maruyama's father, Kunio Maruyama, moved to Manchuria as it was a place of opportunity for adventurous Japanese. And as it would turn out, he would go on to play a role of epic proportions in repatriating this population, as his son Paul would describe in his book, *Escape from Manchuria*.[4] After the war, millions of Japanese soldiers and civilians were scattered across Asia, including Manchuria, a part of China which the Japanese had colonized in 1933.

---

4   Paul K. Maruyama, *Escape from Manchuria* (Tate Publishing & Enterprises, 2014).

In the aftermath of the Pacific War, when communist and nationalist forces fought for control of China, and when Soviet forces attempted to carve out their own part of Northern China, the Japanese were caught between a rock and a hard place—kicked out of their homes by the Soviets, and despised by the Chinese who had suffered under their rule, their bank accounts frozen, their possessions stolen, their hopes of survival slim.

Kunio Maruyama assumed that authorities in Japan would be preoccupied with the changes brought in by the Occupation, and that ultimately, he would have to find a way to convince MacArthur to send US ships to repatriate the Japanese. How he would get to Japan, let alone meet General MacArthur, he had no idea. First, he needed help. The thirty-seven-year-old Maruyama sought the advice of his company's president and was advised to partner with a thirty-one-year-old head of an architectural firm, Hachiro Shinpo. The two agreed that GHQ in Japan needed to know of the abandoned Japanese in Manchuria. Shinpo then introduced a member of his firm, twenty-four-year-old Masamichi Musashi, to join in this effort.

But first they had to get to Japan.

At great risk to their lives, masquerading as Chinese, the three sneaked their way through war zones occupied by the Soviets and Communist Chinese, and were finally able to negotiate with the Nationalist Chinese to allow them safe passage to Japan so they could begin their campaign to repatriate the Japanese in Manchuria.

Despite the tremendous risk of being caught or killed on the way out of China, and the challenge of three unknown Japanese having to figure out a way to navigate the newly established governing structure in Japan, the men were incredibly effective.

They first met in Anshan on October 15, 1945, to sketch out a plan to bring back their countrymen from China. They successfully escaped from China on March 9, 1946, carrying letters from the head of the chairman of the All-Manchuria Japanese Association, an American bishop who headed Manchuria's Catholic Church in Dalian, as well as from Kuomintang officials, who vouched for their mission and helped open doors in Japan. And after a few weeks of publicizing their situation through the press, and meeting with Japanese government officials, the three were able to secure a meeting with General MacArthur on April 5.

Only five weeks later, on May 14, 1946, the first ship transported 1,219 Japanese back from China to Kyushu.

By the time the last ship from China docked in Sasebo,

Kyushu on April 3, 1948, nearly a million and a half Japanese civilians were brought home from Manchuria. Thanks to Maruyama, Shinpo, and Musashi, a generation of families and their progeny were saved and allowed to take part in the revival and economic miracle of Japan. The greatest growth in Japan's population was during the 1950s, at 15.6 percent. The Japanese repatriated from Manchuria and their children helped contribute to that population explosion.

But things could have turned out quite differently that day when the Maruyamas were on the train to Shenyang, the children playing innocently with the Soviet soldiers. When the Maruyamas, the Shinpos, and the then-single Musashi got off the train, Paul's mother, Mary, had the worst of revelations.

"Where's Paul?" she shouted.

Their five-year-old was missing. The dread was evident on all their faces. What could have happened? Happily, just before the incident boiled over into full-blown crisis, Paul was hoisted out of a train window, falling into the arms of his relieved parents. It did not occur to them until afterwards that their mission to find safe passage for the three men to Japan could have ended then and there.

Paul, with his three brothers and mother, Mary, would

return to Japan and reunite with his father, Kunio Maruyama, on January 10, 1947, spending the prior ten months hidden under the protection of the Catholic Church in Dalian. Paul would eventually move to the United States after graduating from a US military dependents' high school in Japan, become a judoka at the American judo powerhouse of San Jose State University, represent the USA at the debut of judo at the 1964 Tokyo Olympics, and coach subsequent judo teams for Team USA.

Millions of Japanese returned to their homeland after being abandoned throughout Asia. And while they were relieved to come home, what they found was a battered and demoralized Japan.

The Maruyama family circa 1950, father Kunio and Robert (standing), mother Mary, Xavier, Joseph and Paul (seated), courtesy of Paul Maruyama

DEVASTATED JAPAN

Maruyama, Shinpo, and Musashi's efforts saved many lives, but the Pacific War still decimated a generation of Japan's youth. Estimates of deaths during the war range from 2.5 to 3.1 million, the majority of which were the young men of the Japanese military. Civilians were not spared, as 550,000 to 800,000 living in Japan and countries throughout Asia died.

In his book, *Embracing Defeat*, John Dower wrote of the utter destruction to Japan's physical landscape, its industrial infrastructure, and its people. According to Dower, 80 percent of all ships, 33 percent of all industrial machine tools, and 25 percent of all motor vehicles and trains in Japan were destroyed. He also wrote that sixty-six major cities in Japan were bombed by American planes, on average destroying 40 percent of those geographies and leaving 30 percent of their populations without homes. The three largest cities were rendered wastelands with the homeless rates at 89 percent for Nagoya, 57 percent for Osaka, and 65 percent for Tokyo.[5]

The end of the war did not bring joy, only momentary relief, as the vast majority of Japanese citizens entered a new phase of open competition for food and security; any elation over the repatriation of 5 million countrymen was quickly overwhelmed by feelings of shame and frustration.

MacArthur's Japan, an early firsthand account of those days written by AP journalist, Russell Brines, describes

---

5   John Dower, *Embracing Defeat: Japan in the Wake of World War II* (New York: Norton, 2000), ebook location 571-584.

a Japan unrecognizable today. It includes this portrayal of the repatriation of Japanese soldiers and civilians from abroad.

Men, women and children—tired and dirty—plodded off the ship, wound past the American sentry and pushed up a hill toward a weather-beaten building. They stood like cattle while doctors deloused them, then walked to the railroad station. As they waited for trains, gloomy and apprehensive, commuters eyed them stiffly before hurrying away. Only relatives gave them a smile or a soft word. They soon learned the rest of Japan was too busy—or just unconcerned—to give much thought to the cycle of fate that had deposited them like rubbish on their nation's doorstep.

Jammed, filthy trains took them to all parts of the homeland. Some had been away as long as eight years. They returned to blowsy cities, tiny villages, or drab farms; to the narrow, contained life they had left for conquest. Many found stony neighbors, silently condemning them for sharing in defeat or for failing to die, as custom decreed. Others encountered resentment from people miserly over food and patched clothing. Some located only ashes where their homes had been and only vagueness when they searched for missing relatives.

The sifting of lives continued, day by day, behind paper-curtained little homes. Men returned to find their "widows" remarried. Some wives had become streetwalkers, through necessity or restlessness. Women had lost some of their obedience and most of their patience. The fabric of prearranged, loveless marriages was too weak in many cases to survive long separation and irritable reconciliation. For the first time, women became complainants in divorce suits; including one whose husband brought back a native wife and two children from Borneo.

Jobs were scarce, money useless, and the new life confusing. Those who returned swaggering, found no one willing to cringe before them, as had subject peoples. Those who came back ashamed and penitent found no pity. Only the opportunists profited, the men who had kept their eyes open to all the sharp practices they saw abroad.[6]

Dower referred to this postwar malaise as *kyodatsu*, a Japanese word for the collective depression that fell on the country. After all, when the emperor got on the radio on August 15, 1945, to announce that the war had ended, they had not only heard the voice of a divine being for the first time; after years of being told of the need to fight to the end, they were suddenly told to stop their resistance, and to go on living and work toward Japan's recovery.

The immediate meaning of 'liberation' for most Japanese was not political but psychological. Surrender—and,

---

6   Russell Brines, *MacArthur's Japan* (J. B. Lippincott Company, 1948), 102-103.

by association, the Allied victory, the American army of occupation itself—liberated them from death. Month after month, they had prepared for the worst; then, abruptly, the tension was broken. In an almost literal sense, they were given back their lives. Shock bordering on stupefaction was a normal response to the emperor's announcement, usually followed quickly by an overwhelming sense of relief. But that sense of relief all too often proved ephemeral.[7]

The late 1940s was a very difficult period for the Japanese. They had lost their family members, their homes, and to a great extent their identities. They were in need of the basics to survive: food, shelter, and medicine. And they had no assurances about the future. Will Japan recover? Will my family survive?

And yet, by the very existence of an Olympic Games in Tokyo, Japan had answered those questions resoundingly. This was a hopeful Japan welcoming the world to its shores and willing its national heroes to great achievement. But could they will Kaminaga to victory?

---

7   John Dower, *Embracing Defeat: Japan in the Wake of World War II* (New York: Norton, 2000), ebook location 1231.

Emperor at opening ceremony, courtesy of PHOTO KISHIMOTO

THE INEVITABLE

For much of the match, the two judoka maintained strong grips on one another, Kaminaga's uniform already peeled open to the waist, and Geesink streaming sweat down his face and neck. Both made attempts early on to find the leverage to flip or take down the other, but for the most part, the two stood upright as the clock ticked.

As he explained to reporters after the match, Geesink had decided to change tactics. In previous bouts, he came out more aggressively, looking to win early. But in the finals, "I changed my plan. In the first five or six minutes, I would just try to get a reserve, just get ahead on points.

Then Kaminaga would be forced to attack and I would have the advantage."[8]

As the clock approached ten minutes, Kaminaga went on the offensive, thrusting his left leg in between Geesink's legs with the intent to throw the larger man with an *uchi mata*. Unfortunately, the move backfired as Geesink dragged Kaminaga to the mat and rolled him around until he had Kaminaga in a *kesa gatame*—a headlock. An inescapable headlock. As a report in the *Japan Times* stated, "It was like a ten-ton vise that made Kaminaga's counter action totally futile."[9]

Anton Geesink and Akio Kaminaga, courtesy of PHOTO KISHIMOTO

8   AP, "Anton's Strategy Threw Foe," *Pacific Stars & Stripes*, October 25, 1964.

9   Kiyoaki Murata, "Judo Champ Geesink Overpowers Kaminaga," *The Japan Times*, October 24, 1964.

Another Japanese novelist, Renzaburo Shibata, witnessed this match and wrote that at the moment Kaminaga went down, thousands of spectators let out a "gasp of desperation."[10]

After holding Kaminaga immobile for the required thirty seconds, Geesink was declared the winner. Dutch supporters attempted to rush the mat in celebration, but Geesink immediately jumped to his feet and kept them back with stern hand waves and a scowl. The Dutchman, who had trained for years in Japan, knew this was no time to add insult to injury.

The two judoka found their places at the middle of the mat, stoically kneeled, straightened up their uniforms, stood, and bowed to each other. The crowd politely applauded and then went quiet.

Maruyama watched the scene with ambivalence.

> On the one hand, I felt that Geesink's win made the sport of judo a truly international sport and no longer simply a Japanese martial art. On the other hand, I knew what a heartbreak the loss meant to all Japanese who had finally come out from under the cloud that had been present since Japan's defeat in World War II, and judo was the

---

10   Sankei Shimbun, October 24, 1964, in Tokyo Olympic—*Bungakusha ni Yoru Tokyo Gorin Zenkiroku* (Kodansha; 2015) 175.

one Olympic sport Japan expected, or was even obligated, to win in the Tokyo Games. I happened to go by the athletes' dressing room after the match, and I saw several Japanese students, mostly Meiji University judoka, crying their hearts out.

Dutch swimmer and two-time silver medalist at the 1964 Tokyo Olympics, Ada Kok, was invited by the Dutch National Olympic Committee to watch this particular judo final and was taken aback by the moment.

I had just turned 16, so I accepted this invitation as a matter of course. It was just a fight to me at the time. But on reflection, I realized I was watching a culture shock of sorts, going throughout Japan. The Budokan was silent. Quiet. I could hear people crying. It was like a solar eclipse had suddenly blackened out all of Japan. It was a feeling of doom.

CHAPTER 2

THE COLD WAR

A BLESSING, A DISTRACTION, AND A DEFECTION

TUNNEL 57—A LOVE STORY

At the 1964 Tokyo Olympics, East and West Germany competed as one team, under a single flag, Beethoven's Ninth Symphony ("Ode to Joy") their national anthem. This was a compromise brokered by the International Olympic Committee (IOC), which resulted in a sporting détente of sorts, allowing for athletes to be granted visas to either nation. But the unity of the "German" team was more of a mirage, as geopolitical realities created distance between athletes from East and West.

After the Berlin Wall went up in 1961, the flow of athletes between the two Germanys diminished greatly. The IOC and the respective East and West German Olympic officials worked hard to reestablish the unity, negotiating over a thousand hours across ninety-six meetings to ensure that Germany would march as one at the 1964 Tokyo Olympics, as they had done since the 1956 Games in Melbourne. But they would no longer have combined teams as they had in the past. For example, in field hockey, the East German squad defeated the West German squad; there was no combined team as there had been in previous Olympiads.[11]

Tokyo would also be the last time the Germans would maintain any semblance of unity. At the 1968 Mexico City Olympics, the East and West Germans would march under two separate flags.

In October 1964, the Iron Curtain was a philosophical metaphor for the Cold War, but the Berlin Wall that separated East and West Berlin was a very real barrier. Only days before the opening of the Tokyo Olympics, it was reported that fifty-seven people had successfully escaped from East Berlin to West Berlin through a tunnel dug under the wall, "believed to be one of the biggest mass escapes since the Red Wall was erected in the summer of 1961."[12]

11   G.A. Carr, "The Involvement of Politics in the Sporting Relationships of East and West Germany, 1945-1972," *Journal of Sport History* 7, no. 1 (Spring 1980): 45-49.

12   AP, "47 East Berliners Tunnel Way to West," *Pacific Stars & Stripes*, October 7, 1964.

During the existence of the Berlin Wall, from 1961 to 1989, around 5,000 people escaped in a variety of ways—balloons, tightrope, and other means, as well as tunnels. A civil engineering student in East Berlin named Joachim Neumann played a significant role in planning and executing the early tunnel escapes.

Living in East Berlin, Neumann sneaked past border guards to West Berlin posing as a Swiss student in 1961. And while Neumann continued his studies in West Berlin, he also began to apply his new knowledge to the building of tunnels under the Wall.

Neumann got his start in Cold War tunneling on a team that built an underground passageway in 1962, resulting in the successful escape of twenty-nine people over two days, September 14 and 15. Neumann had a girlfriend, Christa Gruhle, in East Berlin, but was unable to inform her in time of the day of escape. But his experience with Tunnel 29, as it is now known, encouraged Neumann to believe that he would have other opportunities to bring his girlfriend to freedom.

Unfortunately, the next attempt ended in calamity as the East German secret police uncovered the existence of the tunnel in progress. One of the people arrested was Gruhle, who was caught trying to escape. She was then held for eight months before being sentenced to two years in prison. Neumann was particularly pained by this arrest, as Gruhle had attempted her escape in order to be with him.

Neumann continued to work on tunnel projects from the West Berlin side, including the one that was completed in October 1964. The plan was to smuggle East Germans through the tunnel on October 3. Just days before, Neumann got a letter from Gruhle, who had just been released from prison and was back in East Berlin. Neumann searched frantically to find someone who could get word to his girlfriend that she had to prepare immediately to sneak through the tunnel. After finally finding a friend to contact her, Neumann rushed to the tunnel, as it was his role to open it, greet the East Berliners at the entrance, and guide them to freedom.

Little by little, escapees made their way to Strelitzer Strasse 55 in East Berlin, where an apartment building near the Wall hid the entrance to the tunnel. The East Berliners would take off their shoes, slip silently down a hallway, cross a courtyard, and then descend into a hole located in an unused outdoor toilet room. Once in the tunnel, sixty centimeters high, and a meter wide, the escapees crawled their way to freedom to a bakery in Bernauer Strasse in West Berlin.

To gain access to the secret tunnel, the escapees first

had to whisper the code word—"Tokyo"—selected by the tunnel builders as the Olympics were being held that month.

Every ten minutes, another person or another family would make their way through the East Berlin entrance, Neumann fully aware that the next person could be an East German soldier. "We all had pistols," he said. "There had been shootings before." Too busy to be fearful, too focused on the here and now, Neumann was surprised to see a young woman appear before him. It was Christa Gruhle.[13]

Over two nights on October 3 and 4, fifty-seven people escaped to West Berlin through "Tunnel 57" before East German guards discovered it and shut it down. A few months later, Neumann and Gruhle married, and stayed together for forty years until she passed away in 2004.[14]

A BLESSING

As the escapees of Tunnel 57 can attest to, the Cold War conflict put peoples' lives at stake. It was a time when Americans built air-raid shelters in their backyards, people were executed for sharing military secrets, and

---

13   Justin Huggler, "An Audacious Dig for Freedom Beneath the Berlin Wall," *The Telegraph* (February 3, 2018).

14   Simon Watts, "Tunneling Under the Berlin Wall to Save My Girlfriend," *BBC,* May 9, 2014.

the missile crisis in Cuba between the United States and the Union of Soviet Socialist Republics held the world in a state of paralyzing fear as we stared the possibility of nuclear war in the face.

And yet, for Japan, the Cold War was a most unusual blessing.

At the end of the Pacific War, the Japanese economy was a shambles, with its industrial base destroyed, millions of people homeless and out of work, and inflation raging at 100 percent annually. To tame inflation, the director of the US government's Bureau of the Budget, Joseph Dodge, was sent to Japan to stabilize its weakened economy. His policies of austerity reined in inflation but also triggered bankruptcies, increased unemployment, and depressed consumer spending.

On top of that, the industrial base of Japan was severely weakened. That which survived the bombing raids by allied forces at the end of the war was dismantled and shipped off to allies of the United States as war reparations. And even if a Japanese manufacturer still had its machinery intact, they were often forbidden from using it.

Kuroda Precision Industries manufactured precision gauges for the famed Zero fighters during the war but had to resort to a totally different business in the new postwar reality.

"They took the extremely punitive measure of putting a freeze on all equipment," said the company's former president, Shoichi Kuroda. "How could machinery manufacturers like us operate without equipment? So we ended up transforming our operations and producing salt. When electricity is applied to sea water, the water evaporates and leaves the salt behind. Salt was very much in demand after the war. I had heard that banks would lend you money if you brought them salt. I'm serious!"[15]

But in the late 1940s, as Supreme Commander of the Allied Powers (SCAP), General Douglas MacArthur was working to implement reforms to turn Japan into a democracy while at the same time implementing punitive measures to ensure it would not become a military power again. Fortunately, the geopolitical dynamics of the Cold War were conspiring to aid a Japanese economy on life support.

On June 25, 1950, armed forces from North Korea invaded the South, sparking a three-year military conflict, not only between the Koreas, but also among the United States,

---

15   "NHK, "A Portrait of Postwar Japan Part 1: Economic Miracle, Shimomura's Theory," YouTube video. Posted April 2017.

which supported South Korea; and communist China, as well as the Soviet Union, which supported the North.

With a substantial American military presence already in Japan to support SCAP's efforts to democratize the country, and a growing realization that a weak Japan would only make America's ability to thwart a growing communist presence in Asia more difficult, the American government realized they had to reverse course on Japan. Despite the peace Constitution, authored by a committee that answered to MacArthur, and which renounced both war and the maintenance of any form of military, the American government now began to source products and services from Japan for the Korean War effort.

Special procurement orders suddenly began filtering throughout Japan's existing manufacturing base—orders for metal products, electronic equipment, fuel and oil, textiles and clothing, medicine, trucks, construction equipment, paper products, food and drink. The Korean War was a lifeline to Japanese industry, stimulating employment and putting cash in the hands of workers across the nation. Between 1950 and 1953, over 2 billion US dollars were pumped into the Japanese economy, more than the total amount of aid Japan had received in the first six years of the Allied Occupation.

Toyota's president at the time said that their production

climbed 40 percent thanks to the special procurement orders. "Those orders were Toyota's salvation. I felt a mingling of joy for my company and a sense of guilt that I was rejoicing over another country's war."[16]

Procurement orders were also music to the ears of the head of Kuroda Precision Industries.

"We got busy!" said president Shoichi Kuroda. "We were making gauges for 108mm Howitzers. We had mixed feelings about it because munitions production was banned in principle. But the work put our plants back to life. At long last, the sound of machinery running could be heard in our factories once again."[17]

16   John Dower, *Embracing Defeat: Japan in the Wake of World War II* (New York: Norton, 2000), ebook location 9810.

17   "NHK. A Portrait of Postwar Japan Part 1: Economic Miracle, Shimomura's Theory," YouTube video. Posted April 2017.

Cauldron under construction, courtesy of PHOTO KISHIMOTO

The economy continued to chug along after the flood of procurement orders dried up and kicked into high gear heading into the 1960s. When Hayato Ikeda replaced Nobusuke Kishi as prime minister in 1960, he launched the country on a plan to double the income of all employed workers by the end of the decade. The government invested significantly in heavy industry and infrastructure and supported the creation of an export engine that helped double workers' incomes in only seven years, fueling a consumer economy that had been dormant for decades.

When foreigners arrived at Haneda Airport in 1964, they could get to downtown Tokyo in only fifteen minutes on the brand-new monorail. While getting around town in a taxi to go buy nifty cameras and timepieces, they climbed the ramps to a network of highways that sped them along the sides of a growing number of gleaming office buildings. And if they wanted to get to Osaka, they could ride in style on the fastest train in the world, the Bullet Train, which debuted only nine days before the opening of the Olympics.

For those caught up in the Games and the surrounding excitement of Japan's progress in everything from consumer goods to gee-whiz technological innovation, the Cold War may have seemed a distant rumor, but to a few hundred on hand for the event, the Cold War had significant consequences.

YOU HAVE TO BE IN IT TO WIN IT

Shin Keum Dan, the North Korean star of the women's 400- and 800-meter events and the unofficial world record holder in the latter, had only precious minutes before the North Korean team left Tokyo. Her father, Shin Mun Jun, who was separated from his daughter during the Korean War, was hoping to take advantage of the Olympics to see her compete over the two weeks of competition.

Separated from her father at the age of twelve, both Shin and her mother in North Korea had thought her father was dead. But the father had read a newspaper story about his daughter's success at the 1963 sports tournament in Indonesia and told his story to a South Korean newspaper. That story was picked up in a North Korean paper, thus alerting the daughter and mother to her father's whereabouts.

Unfortunately, after fourteen years of separation, they were allowed to share only five minutes together at the Korean Kaikan Hall in Tokyo just prior to her boarding the team bus. Shin Keum Dan and her father were caught in the middle of a geopolitical conflict. On Monday, October 5, 1964, the North Korean team disembarked from a Soviet ship in Niigata and took a train to Tokyo to participate in the XVIII Olympiad. On Friday, October 9, the North Korean delegation made an about-face and returned to North Korea, only one day prior to the start of the Games.

On the same day, the entire Indonesian delegation also left Japan, joining North Korea in a boycott of the Olympics, a possibility that had been brewing for months.

To go back, in 1962, Indonesia had hosted a regional sporting event called the Asian Games. Because of Indonesian President Sukarno's establishment of a One

China policy favoring the communist People's Republic of China, and his Islamic country's adoption of a pro-Arab stance, he refused entry of athletes from Israel and Taiwan. Frowning on blatant political posturing getting in the way of the broadest level of national inclusion, International Olympic Committee president Avery Brundage suspended Indonesia's membership in the IOC, the first time a member had ever been suspended. In reaction to that, Indonesia organized the GANEFO Games, "The Games of the New Emerging Forces," which boldly stated that politics and sports should indeed be intertwined.

The first GANEFO Games were held in Jakarta, Indonesia, and included 2,700 athletes from sixty-six nations. While most of the larger nations, like the Soviet Union, did not send their top athletes, Indonesia and North Korea did.

Holding out hope that Indonesia would alter its stance if he held out a carrot, Brundage reinstated Indonesia's membership in the IOC. In the end, it came down to the international sports federations, which establish the standards for qualifications to the Olympics. On September 21, 1964, the international governing boards of swimming (FINA) and athletics (IAAF) ruled that athletes who participated in the GANEFO Games would not be eligible for the Olympics in those events.

Unfortunately, a significant number of swimmers as

well as track and field athletes were on the Indonesian and North Korean teams. Instead of simply removing GANEFO participants, North Korea and Indonesia decided to pull their entire teams out of Japan.

It must have been an incredible disappointment to Indonesian and North Korean athletes—to arrive in Tokyo only to be told to return home on the eve of the opening ceremonies. For Shin Keum Dan and her father, it must have been devastating, as this Mainichi report conveys:

> As the group's bus was about to start for the station to catch the train, the father and daughter firmly grasped their hands. With swollen eyes, they exchanged brief remarks like "Are you all right?" and "Let us exchange letters."[18]

And the father watched as the bus took his daughter away. Except for those fleeting minutes, they were not to meet again. "My daughter gave me ginseng as a gift, but the best gift for me was the warm, warm tears she shed when she recognized me," said the father.[19]

Shin would continue to run, in fact she would compete in the second and last GANEFO Games in 1966 in Cambo-

---

18 Kenji Mitoma, "Shins Reunited After 14 Years of Separation," *The Mainichi Daily News*, October 10, 1964.

19 UPI, "Reunion of Shins Sets Off ROK 'Brotherhood' Drive," *The Japan Times*, October 15, 1964.

dia, but never in an international competition that would recognize her results.

The angst of the Indonesian and North Korean athletes was heart-wrenching. But a day later it was forgotten by the rest of the world amidst the pomp and pageantry of the opening ceremonies. The Games were on.

US-USSR

Jerry Shipp didn't like to lose. He didn't shake hands with opponents after games. He admitted that a basketball game to him was war, and in the heat of battle, he wasn't a good sport. A shooting guard on the US men's basketball team, Shipp had a chip on his shoulder, one that had grown since his days in an orphanage in Tipton, Oklahoma.

The two-meter-tall shooting guard, whose unorthodox shooting form was often deadly from a distance, Shipp became the highest scorer ever for Southeastern State College (now known as Southeastern Oklahoma State University). Drafted by the New York Knicks in 1959, Shipp decided that he needed a steady job and higher pay than what he could get in the NBA. He opted for work at the oil company Phillips, which also had a team in the corporate league, the now-defunct National Industrial Basketball League (NIBL). He would go on to lead the

Phillips 66ers to three consecutive championships in the NIBL, while also playing on the national men's basketball squad.

In 1962, Shipp was on the US squad that played the Soviet national team in Lubbock, Texas, in an exhibition match. In contrast to the 1960 squad that featured future hall-of-famers Jerry West, Oscar Robertson, Walt Bellamy, and Jerry Lucas, the 1962 team prepping for the Tokyo Games was considered a team of no-names, "a second-rate representative for Uncle Sam," not only losing to the Soviets 66-63, but ending the game in unsportsmanlike fashion.

Sam Blair, a sports columnist from the Dallas Morning News, wrote that in the last moments of the game, the Soviet center, Alexsandr Petrov, and Shipp were fighting over possession of the ball when Shipp swung arms and elbows clipping Petrov across the chin and sending him to the hard court.

> It was a pretty shameful moment for the US for Shipp swung in a fit of anger after retreating madly to tie up Petrov, who had slipped free down court in the last hectic seconds to take a high-lob pass and was preparing to sink a simple layup. Fortunately, the Russian had a cooler temper or more self-discipline than Shipp did.[20]

---

20   Sam Blair, "Red Faces in Lubbock" *The Dallas Morning News*, November 23, 1962.

As Shipp recalled, famed sports columnist Blackie Sherrod wrote that he was trying to start World War III.

No US team had ever lost a basketball game in the Olympics through 1960. And yet, just as the Tokyo Olympics were about to start, the US press was predicting that the streak would end. And if any team was going to do it, it would have to be the Soviet team, runners-up to the US in the previous three Olympics.

The coach of the US men's basketball team was Hank Iba, a basketball legend. He coached teams to NCAA championships in 1945 and 1946, and to medals in the Olympics in 1964, 1968, and 1972. And yet, even legends get criticized. "The 12 men selected yesterday for the October duty in Tokyo have the best chance in history to lose one," wrote columnist George Meyers.[21]

Iba knew he didn't have the firepower of the 1960 team. "Our big problem is that we have no one man who'll get us twenty points every game," he pointed out. "So it has to be a team effort. But when a team has played together as short a time as this one has, it's bound to get sloppy at times."[22] Sloppy, yes, but it did not bode well that the team lost its last two exhibition games in the United

---

21 Georg Myers, "The Yank Dribblers—A Shock in Tokyo?" *The Seattle Daily Times*, April 6, 1964.

22 Tim Horgan, "U. S. Hoopsters Feel Pressure," *Traveler Sports*, October 21, 1964.

States prior to shipping off to Hawaii for a training camp just before the Olympics.

Fortunately, Coach Iba was one of the toughest, most well-prepared coaches of his time. Center Luke Jackson said that the team was constantly practicing. "Coach Iba wouldn't let up. When we first came in the locker room, he gave each of us a notepad and said, 'I want you to learn these plays. Those who don't learn, won't play.' And then he walked out of the room. We practiced those plays. And those who didn't learn them, didn't play."

"Those five-hour practices a day—those were tough," recalled forward Jeff Mullins. "He had his Iba-isms. If you had a turnover he would say in his raspy voice, 'Can't have that, boys. Can't have that.'"

The US team crushed the team from South Korea 116-50 in one of the early contests of the Tokyo Olympics. Jackson said that after the game, "Iba took us to practice and worked us until our feet fell off. He said that we didn't rebound well. He was just putting it on our mind that every game was important. You have to do things the same way every time. I'm sure we were hot-dogging against the Koreans. And we realized that this guy was serious."

Prior to the finals, the American men's team didn't lose, despite what many had predicted. And so, the USSR and the USA teams both went into the gold medal round undefeated, playing for geopolitical bragging rights and Olympic glory at the beautiful Kenzo Tange-designed Gymnasium Annex in Yoyogi.

In the first eight minutes, the Americans played sluggishly as the Soviets jumped to a lead. Iba admitted jitters. "I've been in this business a long time," he said to reporters after the game. "I know if you get so sure you're going to win, you usually get knocked on your bottom. But we never talked about it."

Toward the middle of the first half, Jackson woke up, grabbing rebounds and sinking baskets. And then, the rest of the team got going. Joe Caldwell started pouring in points. He was joined by Bill Bradley (he of Princeton, the Knicks, and the US Senate), Larry Brown (he of the countless university and pro coaching roles), Walt Hazzard, and Shipp, who led the US team in scoring average in the tournament and did not cause World War III.

In the end, the US men's team continued its dominance, defeating the Soviet Union 73-59, and registering its forty-seventh straight victory since basketball became an Olympic sport at the 1936 Berlin Games. It was one of the last of the USA's thirty-five total gold medals gathered at the Tokyo Olympics and marked the first time that the US won more gold medals than the Soviet Union since the powerful communist nation was allowed into the Olympics in 1952.

But the Cold War was not on Shipp's mind when the gold medal was placed around his neck. Shipp had played countless times against the Soviets, knew them inside out, and would have run through a brick wall to defeat them. But it was not triumph over the Russians that caused his breath to shorten or his heart to tremor. It was the realization that the long climb out of his childhood, one filled with hurt, insecurity, and loneliness, was over.

As he stood on the medal stand, waiting for his gold medal, memories of the orphanage where he grew up and the school he attended flooded his mind's eye. He remembered his high school algebra teacher, Miss Maynard, who, instead of nurturing him, told him he was never going to learn anything. Out of frustration, Shipp once completed an algebra test by putting a zero on it, and submitting it as is. The teacher told him, "You will never amount to anything. You'll be in jail one day."

And so, at the moment the twenty-seven-year-old bent at the waist to receive his gold medal, the volcano at the pit of his stomach, roiling with the bilious lava of his youth, erupted.

I straightened up and I saw the camera pointing at me with the red light on, and I shouted, "Old Lady Maynard, I hope you're watching, 'cause I made something out of myself!" I never forgot it. I was still angry. My teammate, George Wilson, was standing next to me and asked me what that was all about. But I never told him.

I now realize that Lotus Maynard played such a big part in my life. I just got to thinking that my anger was hurting nobody but me. I realized, in fact, that she drove me to success. Now I go back and I say, "Mrs. Maynard, thank you."

DREAMING OF AMERICA

Andras Toro never got that chance to stand on the podium in Tokyo. His bid for a medal fell just short—a fact that would change his life forever.

Four years earlier, it was a different story. He stood on the podium at the 1960 Rome Olympics, with his partner, veteran canoeist, Farkas Imre. The two Hungarians wore grim faces, just losing out on the silver medal to the Italian team, who stood slightly higher, giddy to do unexpectedly well in their home country.

Toro was twenty years old at the time and could imagine competing in future Olympics. But Imre was at the end of his career. He had already won a bronze medal at the

1956 Melbourne Olympics, and to be nipped at the line by an upstart Italian team was devastating to the veteran.

"Paddling back to the boat house, I finally congratulated Farkas," wrote Toro in his soon-to-be published autobiography—*An Olympic Defector's Chronicle*. "He expressed his disappointment and said that this was his last chance. I wondered if I would have another chance at Olympic gold."

One benefit of winning a medal on the Hungarian Olympic team was permission to see whatever Olympic events remained, and to go wherever in Italy he wanted. Toro witnessed the prowess of track stars Wilma Rudolph, Rafer Johnson, and Abebe Bikila, as well as the brash boxer Cassius Clay, and cheered on his Hungarian teammates at other events. He went on tours of Napoli, Pompei, and Capri. For a young man from a socialist economy, who yearned for the freedom and bounty of the West, Toro was in heaven.

And yet all good things must come to an end, and back to Hungary and factory work he returned. Fortunately, Toro was invited to a canoeing competition in Potsdam, East Germany, a few months later. The Hungarian team did well, a fitting end to a successful year. But what the paddlers were really excited about was an upcoming trip to Berlin. In 1960, that city was divided into quarters based on a postwar agreement carved out between the Allies and the Soviet Union. The quarter that drew Toro's interest was the American sector.

Hungary was then a communist nation in the Soviet sphere, and thus its citizens were generally not allowed into West Berlin. But one of Toro's teammates spoke German, and their understanding was that the border crossing from the Soviet sector to the American sector at that time was not so tight.

They got on the train. And when they approached West Berlin, they showed the conductor their Hungarian passports, and that was that. "We looked at each other. It was smooth sailing to West Berlin."

The Hungarians' first order of business was to exchange Hungarian forints for US dollars. The sight of the bills took Andras Toro back to the day as a child when he first saw American money, when his father came home with a dollar bill.

In those days, Western material goods and symbols were banned in Hungary. Holding US currency could land a Hungarian in prison. And yet, Toro remembers how his father held that single dollar bill in his hands with glee, as though it contained secrets beyond its monetary value.

Now Andras had a few dollars in hand, and he was in the city that was as close to being part of America as you could get in Europe—West Berlin. With its strong US military and diplomatic presence, not to mention the commercial influences, West Berlin had a thick overlay of Americana.

The first thing Toro wanted to do was have a bottle of Coca Cola. Despite the relatively high price of twenty-five cents, he had to have this sip of freedom. "I gave it a shot. It tasted awful, just like the throat medication my mother used to give me in the winter time when I had strep throat."

Fortunately, there were other marvelous things to see and do. And what better taste of American pop culture could one have at that time than *West Side Story*, a Broadway musical turned Hollywood film, with superstar Natalie Wood. "It was playing in one of the theaters with the marquee so illuminated it was almost blinding. We had heard of this movie and had listened to the soundtrack through the Radio Free Europe station. We had to see this picture." So the Hungarians spent a chunk of their per diem on tickets, "but it was worth the price."

Then there was the shopping. Not only was it a joy for Hungarians to buy clothes in a non-communist country so that they could show off the latest Western fashions back home, much of the merchandise could be resold in Hungary for a considerable profit. Toro bought wristwatches, stockings, and razor blades with the few dollars he had left.

Toro had a fascination for the West, particularly America. And as he walked around the bright lights of Kurfürstendamm Strasse, he had a thought: how wonderful would it be one day to live in the United States?

TO DEFECT OR NOT TO DEFECT—THAT WAS THE QUESTION

At the 1964 Tokyo Olympics, the kayakers and canoeists landed at Haneda Airport like most other Olympians, but then were whisked off to Sagamihara, about sixty kilometers west of Tokyo. The competitions for the canoeists and kayakers were to be held at Lake Sagami, a man-made reservoir in an idyllic setting developed for tourists.

To Andras Toro, it was dreamlike:

> Lake Sagami was a magical place with all the oriental beauty we had only seen before in magazines...the morning mist that rose along the shoreline was beautifully surreal.

Andras Toro at Lake Sagami, courtesy of Andras Toro

It was the perfect setting for Cold War intrigue.

Since the 1956 Hungarian Revolution, Toro and his friends in the Honved Canoe Club in Budapest had given serious thought to defecting from their country, as long as it was under the hammer (and sickle) of the Soviet Union. In fact, many of his friends did indeed defect, taking advantage of their participation at the 1956 Melbourne Games.

But Toro didn't go to Melbourne. And his bronze medal finish at the 1960 Rome Olympics only fanned the flames of his desire to win in Tokyo. Competing in the individual 1,000-meter event, Toro had his sights set on the gold. But he also smelled an opportunity—that if he did not win a medal, he would seriously consider defecting to the West.

Just saying that you want to defect, however, doesn't make it happen. There is no defector's manual. Who do you contact? What country would take you? How do you avoid the ears and eyes of your country's minders? Toro spoke almost no English. Who would he even start this conversation with?

And yet, when you want something, as Paulo Coelho famously put it in his novel, *The Alchemist*, "all the universe conspires in helping you to achieve it."

Off the foggy banks of Lake Sagami, the universe began to conspire for Andras Toro.

In the tiny community of Olympic canoeists and kayakers emerged quite unexpectedly a friend of Toro's, Andor Elbert. Friends since their teenage years in the Honved Canoe Club in Budapest, Elbert had defected to Canada eight years prior, and was representing Canada at the 1964 Olympics. Toro, shielded behind his Hungarian minders, was of course never informed that a defector had made the Olympic squad on another nation's team.

Then an American kayaker named Bill Smoke entered the picture. He was at Lake Sagami to compete for the US

Olympic squad, but he was also looking for talent. Smoke lived in Michigan, famous for its lakes and love of boating of all kinds, and he hoped to find someone who could build canoes and kayaks so that he could start a business back home.

Smoke walked over to the Canadian dorms looking for someone who spoke English and happened to have that conversation with Elbert. Smoke wondered if Elbert knew anyone in Canada who might be willing to help him out. As a matter of fact, Elbert did know someone, but he wasn't from Canada.

Elbert told Smoke that his friend Toro was not only good at designing and building boats, he was also hoping to defect from Hungary. Smoke in turn talked with US teammate and then-girlfriend, Marcia Jones, who was in Japan also competing in individual canoeing. She turned out to be a key connection, as her mother was Mary Francis, an attorney, one of two women to graduate from the University of Michigan Law School in 1929. She was also sympathetic to people who had to leave their home countries.

Jones said that when she was ten, they had a DP, or dis- placed person, couple from Latvia stay with them. "The government brought them over here," she said. "My mother sponsored them. They lived at our place. They went to our schools. She wanted to help them out. She was a very generous person and we could afford to help them."

When Jones told her mother about Toro, Mary Francis got to work, contacting the US Embassy in Tokyo to seek their help. According to Smoke, who eventually married Jones, his future mother-in-law was not someone you could say no to easily. Francis was able to set up a meeting for Toro at the Embassy.

So very suddenly, all of the pieces fell into place. Toro was ready to defect, resigned to most likely never seeing his family and home country ever again, but with hopes of starting anew in a new land. All that remained, strangely enough, was for him to lose.

WIN OR LOSE, TORO'S LIFE CHANGES FOREVER

If I win a medal at the 1964 Tokyo Olympics, I will return to Hungary a hero, a medalist in two straight Olympics. If I don't win a medal, I will defect to the United States.

That was the decision-making matrix the twenty-four-year-old Andras Toro created for himself in that third week of October in 1964, as he prepared for his first heat in the individual canoeing competition at the Tokyo Olympics. But it was not as simple a proposition as it seemed.

Let's think about it for a moment. You're a high-performance athlete. You've won the bronze medal at the 1960 Rome Olympics, and you have a chance to establish yourself in the pantheon of Hungarian greats if you medal in Tokyo. You want to win.

Then again, you have dreamed of living overseas ever since your father brought home a world atlas, and you wanted to see the land of canoes and kayaks ever since reading Fennimore Cooper's classic novel, *The Last of the Mohicans*. And since the Soviet crackdown in the aftermath of the 1956 Hungarian Revolution, you wonder whether your aspiring and wandering soul could exist under the authoritarian thumb of the government in power.

But by the same token, can you really leave your family, particularly your dear mother, behind and put them at risk as relatives of a traitor?

In the end, however, Toro kept to his original decision framework: win a medal and return to Hungary; lose and start a new life elsewhere. This is what he confided to his friend Andor Elbert so that they would be ready to put the defection scheme in motion if he were to finish worse than third.

On October 20, the canoeists for the first of two individual 1,000-meter heats lined up on the calm waters of Lake Sagami. Hoping to stay ahead or at least close to his biggest threats, a Bulgarian and a Russian, Toro managed to finish his heat a little less than a second-and-a-half behind the Russian, Yevgeny Penyayev.

Finishing in the top three in the heat qualified Toro for the finals. And yet, his time was only the fourth fastest, which prompted concerns among the coaches that Toro might not have enough to get him a medal.

Two days later, on October 22, Toro lined up for the finals. If he did not medal, he would defect. And yet, Toro knew at that moment, in his heart of hearts, he was there to win.

> I had sacrificed everything during the last couple of years to be here and wanted it really badly. I pushed aside the negative thoughts in my head. I took a couple of deep breaths, and I was ready.[23]

Toro started off strong, keeping an eye on the Russian who had edged Toro in the earlier heat. At the halfway point, he was keeping pace. He made a push, raised his stroke rate, but suddenly things got harder. His lungs burned. His thoughts grew dark. He paddled as best he could with controlled abandon and did well enough to finish third...or so he thought.

23   Andras Toro, *An Olympic Defector's Chronicle.*

Once again he was edged out by the Russian, Penyayev. Unfortunately, the German, Jurgen Eschert, and the Romanian, Andrei Igorov, finished ahead of the Russian. Toro finished fourth, and his fate was sealed.

"I was crushed," Toro wrote in his autobiography. "And then my promise hit me. If I do not win a medal, I would defect. Suddenly I was confronted with reality."

Fortunately, reality came with a plan.

GOING TO AMERICA

Lake Sagami was a good distance away from Tokyo, where most of the Olympic action was, and where most of the attention of the Hungarian minders was focused. The eyes and ears that surveilled things at Lake Sagami were less concerned about the possibility of defection out in the middle of nowhere. And so, when Toro explained to his teammates and coaches that he was heading into Tokyo for some last-second shopping, no one gave it a thought.

At 6 p.m. Toro and Elbert rendezvoused at the train station with the third 'conspirator,' Bill Smoke, and headed quietly into Tokyo and the United States embassy.

On the ride in, which took over an hour, Elbert and

Smoke talked in English, a language that Toro could not understand. He recalled that "everyone was looking at us—three Olympians in their uniforms speaking different languages."

There was a brief meeting with officials at the embassy, Elbert serving as interpreter. As Toro had no money to pay for a plane ticket, Bill Smoke wrote out a check to cover the fare—one way. Shortly afterwards they were on their way to the airport.

Fearing the possibility that news of the defection might already have leaked, embassy officials took pains to escort Toro to the airplane as unobtrusively as possible and put him in a seat where he would have little chance of attracting notice—the cockpit.

For Toro it was an anxious flight, filled with mixed emotions about the past he was leaving behind and concerns about his immediate future. But as his plane descended toward the runway in Anchorage, Alaska, his new friends in the cockpit gave him a present he has treasured ever since. "They each gave me a one dollar bill, and said good luck in America," Toro said. "I didn't have money when I landed except for those four one dollar bills."

Toro thought back to that day when his father first brought

home an American dollar bill, and sparked wonder in a young boy's head about life in another country.

Toro would get his bachelor's and master's degrees in marine engineering at the University of Michigan, become an American citizen, compete in the 1972 Munich and 1976 Montreal Olympics on the US canoeing team, and serve in various roles for subsequent US Olympic teams as coach and administrator.

In 1964, it's safe to say he had no idea of that future. He had only hope.

"I was twenty-four years old, spoke no English, and was heading to a country where I knew almost nobody. All I had in my pocket were those four dollar bills," said Toro. "But for that one moment I felt like the richest man in the world."

CHAPTER 3

FASTER, HIGHER, STRONGER

BOB HAYES AND THE BELIEF THAT ANYTHING'S POSSIBLE

"BULLET" BOB HAYES

Bob Hayes was the clear favorite. No one doubted that the muscular twenty-one-year-old from Jacksonville, Florida, was the fastest man in the world. The only thing that could stop him was himself. Or maybe, Joe Frazier.

Hours before the men's 100-meter sprint finals on October 15, Hayes was sitting quietly in his dorm room trying to keep himself calm. In walked Frazier, the twenty-year-old American boxer, who was also readying for a big fight but, in contrast to Hayes, was a bundle of nerves and could not keep still. "He kept going around the room shadow boxing," remembers Hayes in his autobiography, *Run Bullet Run*.[24]

After rummaging through Hayes's equipment bag and grabbing some gum, the future gold medalist and heavyweight champion of the world bounced out of the room, leaving the sprinter in something of a tizzy.

When it was time, Hayes made his way to the National Stadium to get ready for the 100-meter finals. When he opened his bag, however, he could find only one of his track shoes. He dumped out the contents onto the floor but could still find only his right shoe. "The biggest race of my life, and I was missing a shoe," Hayes reflected.

Tom Farrell, a middle-distance runner on Team USA, happened to walk by, noticed the concern on Hayes's face, and asked what was wrong. After Hayes explained that he was missing his left shoe, Farrell asked what size he wore. Hayes replied size eight, a relatively small size that he knew few of his track teammates would have.

But Hayes, of course, was destined to win this race.

---

24   Bob Hayes with Robert Pack, *Run, Bullet, Run: The Rise, Fall, and Recovery of Bob Hayes* (Harper & Row, 1990), 19.

Farrell told him that he, too, wore size eight, and in fact used the same Adidas 100 shoes. So with borrowed shoes on his feet, Hayes ran the 100-meter final in ten seconds flat, setting a world record.

When Hayes got back to his dorm room, he found his left shoe hiding under the bedspread, where Frazier had accidentally dislodged it when he was looking for gum. Hayes almost got knocked out by the future champion, but Farrell picked him up, and the Bullet set a world record.

But Hayes wasn't done setting speed records.

Six days later, on October 21, Hayes was warming up for the 4x100-meter relay finals with his teammates Paul Drayton, Gerry Ashworth, and Richard Stebbins. This relay team was patched together as injuries to two other American 100-meter finalists, Mel Pender and Trent Jackson, required two 200-meter sprinters—Drayton and Stebbins—to join the team.

There were two preliminary races prior to the finals, and the drop in individual speed and the lack of practice as a team may have shown. No Olympic records, let alone world records were set during those prelims, and in both cases, the US relay team was behind after the first three legs before anchor Hayes took the baton and the heat.

There was concern in Team USA. Would this relay squad hold together and win? Drayton had pulled a leg muscle in his 200-meter competition. He promised to give his best in the finals, but was not confident his leg would hold up.

The gun sounded. Drayton was two meters behind the Polish runner when he handed the baton to Ashworth, who ran well, but did not make a clean baton exchange with Stebbins. So when Stebbins approached the lane to hand the baton to the anchor, Team USA was in fifth place.

Hayes, the future Dallas Cowboys hall-of-fame wide receiver, simply blew by the Jamaican, the Soviet, and the Polish runners in his first thirty meters. Thirty meters later, he shot past the Frenchman. When he broke the tape, Hayes and his teammates set a new world record with a time of thirty-nine seconds flat.

Hayes had already set the individual men's 100-meter world record at ten seconds. And while it is also true that relay legs include a running start, experts say that no one in the fifty-plus years of track history has come close to Hayes's incredible anchor finish. Carl Lewis ran his anchor leg at the 1992 Barcelona Games in 8.85. Usain Bolt ran his fastest anchor leg at the 2010 Penn Relays in 8.71 seconds. But on that cool autumn day in 1964, the last time that running events would be held on the slower cinder tracks, Hayes sped to the tape in 8.5 seconds.[25]

The fastest man in the world?

How about the fastest man of all time.

"WE CAN DO ANYTHING"

The Japanese watched Bob Hayes with fascination. They saw how their fastest sprinter, Hideo Ijima finished the 100-meter semi-finals in 10.6 seconds, well behind Hayes's semi-final time of 9.9 seconds, a world record if it had not been wind-aided. Japanese writer Yuichiro Inoue witnessed the 100-meter competition and remembers seeing Ijima hold up well for thirty meters before the runner's face turned red and his stride fell apart. Clearly, he was not on a physical par with the competition. In contrast, when Hayes ran, said Inoue, it was like "watching a foreign race car shoot down the track."[26]

Journalist Jiro Sato wrote that he would watch Hayes practice at the Oda Field track in the Olympic Village, where the sprinter would repeat his starts over and over

---

25   Pierre-Jean Vazel, "Fastest 4x100m Relay Splits (short list); Speed Endurance," *Speedendurance. com*, May 27, 2014.

26   Yujiro Inoue, "Tada Hitori Hashiru Hayes," Tokyo Shimbun, in *Tokyo Olympic—Bungakusha ni Yoru Tokyo Gorin Zenkiroku* (Kodansha, 2015), 109.

again, running for forty or fifty meters each time before returning for another start. "His movements were slightly different every time. He would watch the starters shoot their pistols just to understand the timing of how each would pull the trigger, so he could adjust his start accordingly. What a great athlete."[27]

Bob Hayes on Oda Field, courtesy of PHOTO KISHIMOTO

In the 1960s, the Japanese economy was heating up. And with the Olympics coming, it was a time when the Olympic motto, *Citius, Altius, Fortius,* Latin for *Faster, Higher, Stronger*, resonated with Japanese government officials, factory workers, students, and athletes alike. The Olympics and athletes like Bob Hayes were setting the bar high. But the Japanese didn't mind. Observing the best and

27   Jiro Satoh, *Tokyo Gorin 1964* (Bunshun Shinsho, 2013), 114.

learning the specific ways to be better was the plan. The sky was the limit.

One of the iconic advertisements of the 1960s was from Morinaga, a sweets manufacturer that marketed an oversized chocolate bar called "Yell." The television commercial jingle for "Yell" blared the phrase "ooki koto wa ii koto da," which loosely translated means, "the bigger the better."

For a nation that was left devastated, homeless, and starving a little less than two decades earlier, it was a time when anything seemed possible.

In 1958, Tokyo Tower was completed, supplanting its model in Paris, the Eiffel Tower, as the tallest tower in the world.

In 1959, Tokyo was selected as host for the 1964 Summer Olympics, beating out Detroit, the engine of America's automobile industry and home to the most powerful companies in the United States, as well as Vienna and Brussels.

When the Olympics commenced in 1964, Tokyo was in the midst of an engineering and construction revolution. Elevated and underground expressways crisscrossed Tokyo. As mentioned in chapter two, one of the few monorails in the world connected Haneda Airport to central Tokyo in only fifteen minutes. And the famed Bullet Train started its run of three-hour trips between Tokyo and Osaka, establishing the global standard for high-speed rail in a country whose rolling stock industry was in tatters at the end of the Pacific War.

Professor Martyn Smith of The School of Oriental and African Studies (SOAS) at the University of London noted that a popular 1960s' magazine for single women, *Shuu-kan Heibon*, would often try to create scenarios to appease the demanding youth market whose expectations for a cooler lifestyle continued to rise. In a January 23, 1964, article called "When Will the Dream Super-Express Begin Running," the writer painted a picture of a young woman taking the day off to ride the Bullet Train to Kyoto for lunch with her boyfriend. After returning home to Tokyo the same way on the same day, she would then, "with a look of innocence, give the excuse of overtime work before joining in her sister's birthday party."[28]

While known for its cheap and shoddy toys and electronics in the 1950s, Westerners woke up to the fact that Japan's cameras, radios, and watches were actually pretty good value for money. Thanks to the hundreds of inspection groups and thousands of Japanese who visited American companies between 1956 and 1966, and the generosity of

---

28 Martyn Smith, (2013) "Between East and West: The Cold War, Japan and the 1964 Tokyo Olympics," *Comparativ* 3 (2013): 100-116.

the American firms to grant patent licenses to the Japanese (thinking that the Japanese companies would never grow strong enough to become competitors), Japanese corporations began to find their footing, establishing a manufacturing and export boom that would come to be known as the Japanese economic miracle.

And while foreign currency flowed into Japan due to booming exports, it was reinvested into targeted domestic industries. And so, in 1964, confidence was high, and the Japanese were eager to welcome the world. Foreigners flooded into Japan for the Olympics. They came in different shapes and sizes, wore unfamiliar dress and spoke in unfathomable tongues. And the Japanese, conscientiously following their long tradition of *omotenashi*, or "hospitality," on the whole embraced them with open arms.

Ted (Theo) Mittet, a twenty-two-year-old Olympic rower from Seattle, Washington, came to Japan with eyes wide open. And he loved it from the start. "Japan is all that I expected and more," he wrote to his parents a week before the start of the Games. "Its people are very friendly to say the least."

Mittet was on a powerful rowing crew that took the bronze medal in the "fours without" competition, an event where each competitor has four rowers without a coxswain. But while many of his teammates on Team USA went home right afterwards, Mittet sold his return ticket to the States and traveled the Western countryside of Japan. And after his journey, he wrote and received many letters.

In a time when people sent telegrams, long-distance phone calls were expensive, and letters took days if not weeks to traverse the seven seas, pens were our keyboards, while boats, planes, and people were our Internet.

It was a time when getting a letter from the postman was a thrill.

> I was very glad to see you letter beside my Mother's Mirror and I cried my father "Received, Received." My father was glad, too. My mother and brother were glad, too. I cried your letter's news all over my friends. I'm afraid you did not write to me soon. But I got your letter. I think happily.

The above was the opening of a letter from a high school student in Matsuyama City, Ehime Prefecture named Katsuhiro Matsuo, overjoyed to get another letter from the young American rower.

Mittet traveled from Tokyo to Yokohama, then on to Kyoto. He passed through Hiroshima, Matsuyama, Beppu, Nagasaki, Niihama, and Nara, before heading back to

Yokohama and Tokyo. During his two months of travel in Japan, he wrote constantly and voluminously to family and friends in the US, as well as new acquaintances he met during the Olympics and his travels. The letters from the Japanese in particular reflect Japan's excitement and curiosity about foreigners and their desire to welcome them to their country and their home.

In a letter to his parents, he wrote about his stopover in Niihama, a town in Western Japan, where he met three Japanese teachers of English. He accepted their offer to teach for three hours in their school, where Mittet became the representative for all life outside Japan. "I was asked questions about the Beatles, dating in America, President Johnson (damn!), and, 'What you think black man?' It was a wonderful experience and I gained much insight on Japanese life and thought."

In cases like these, the Olympics may have given some Japanese the courage to break out of their normally reticent shells and reach out to the world. Mittet was the closest to the outside world for these letter writers, and so they made what was likely an extraordinary effort to write letters in English.

> Dear Theodore, I know how surprised you are to receive this letter from unknown friend in Japan. You visited Silk Center in Yokohama. Where I was working during Olympic

season. You gave me your card. Oh, no. I required you to give it to me. Do you recollect me? If you could, I am glad. Ha Ha. It is difficult for you to recollect me because you met many people, did not you?

—JUNKO AOKI, A STUDENT AT KANAGAWA
UNIVERSITY IN YOKOHAMA

Dear Theodore, You may be surprised to receive this letter from a complete stranger, but I met you at the Toda Rowing Course and talked with you for a few minutes. I gave you a little badge, do you remember me? I'm taking this liberty of writing to you with the sincere hope that you'll accept me as your new Japanese friend.

—EMIKO KOBAYASHI, A HIGH SCHOOL
STUDENT FROM TODA-MACHI, SAITAMA

The Tokyo Olympics were a rush of adrenaline for the Japanese, so many of them amazed and happy to be surrounded by so many foreigners from so many different countries. Just after the end of the Olympics, Mittet met a volunteer interpreter named Teruyo Wakui at Enoshima Station, not far from where she worked translating for the sailors competing in the nearby yachting events. Despite her fatigue, meeting Mittet proved to be another rush for this young woman.

When I happened to meet you at Enoshima station, I was rather tired after twenty days' work. But I was so glad to meet you and to speak with you. In yachting game, there was no competition as you. Most of all the competitors of yachting were rather gentle and kind, and even the younger men were not as young as you. You are so young and full of dream and curiosity to many things of Japan.

After twenty days in yacht harbor, I suddenly remembered that youth is more wonderful than any other thing in this world. We can do anything without money, as we are young. And though you say you don't have courage, I think you have enough courage to do anything that you want.

THAT was Japan in 1964.

WRESTLING GOLD RUSH

Japan had high hopes for wrestling at the 1964 Tokyo Olympics. And in fact, Japanese wrestlers won five gold medals, becoming overnight heroes for their country. Osamu Watanabe, famously known as The Animal, won an incredible 189 consecutive wrestling matches in his career, including his gold medal match in the freestyle featherweight class.

But one of the lesser known of the wrestling heroes was Yojiro Uetake, who moved to the United States in 1963 and competed for Oklahoma State University. Uetake wasn't asked to come back to Japan to compete for the

Olympic team as he was no longer on the Japanese radar, so he made his way back to Tokyo in the early summer of 1964. When he arrived at the training camp where wrestlers would be selected to represent Japan in the Olympics, Uetake said his sudden appearance made others uncomfortable.

Yojiro Uetake, courtesy of PHOTO KISHIMOTO

The selection process required him to wrestle six others competing in the bantamweight division. And the competition was strong: Hiroshi Ikeda (1963 bantamweight world champion), Tomiaki Fukuda (1965 bantamweight world champion), Masaaki Kaneko (1966 featherweight world champion), and Takeo Morita (1969 featherweight world champion). But the Japanese from Oklahoma swept through the competition and finished 6-0, sealing his selection to the 1964 Olympics.

At the start of the Tokyo Olympics, the wrestler from the Soviet Union, Aydin Ibrahimov, was considered a strong favorite to win gold in the bantamweight class of the free-style wrestling competition. As it turned out, Uetake met Ibrahimov in the semi-finals and in the heat of the battle, Uetake's left shoulder popped out of its socket. His coach pressed hard on Uetake's arm and popped his shoulder back in. "I didn't feel anything," Uetake said, but he went on to tackle Ibrahimov twice to win 2-0. "When you are in the Olympics, tension is very high. I was simply so excited I didn't feel any pain. Of course, after it was all done, it hurt a lot!"

Uetake had plowed through the competition to this point. But to win the gold, Uetake had to defeat Huseyin Akbas of Turkey, the reigning 1962 World Wrestling Champion. And to that day, no Japanese had ever beaten him. Uetake understood that he only needed a tie to win the gold medal, but in such cases, a wrestler can become passive, he thought, so he needed to get aggressive.

Uetake wanted to take Akbas down by grabbing his left leg, but was cautious because Akbas was fast and known for turning that attack to his advantage and flipping his opponent. It seemed to Uetake that Akbas was staying away while Uetake was trying to find the right opening. In the second round, the referee briefly stopped the fight to warn Uetake to attack, and gave Akbas a point. That was the only point Uetake had given up so far in his Tokyo Olympic competition, but with little time left he had now fallen behind.

BORN IN JAPAN, MADE IN THE USA

The Japanese in the lower weight classes were feared for their speed and strength, which the press would duly note. "They are as pliable as cats and as strong as bulls. Again and again it becomes obvious that the Japanese win because of their speedy reactions and their enormous leg strength."[29]

American wrestler, Dave Auble faced off against Uetake in the semi-finals, but he said he was simply outplayed. "Everything I tried to do, he was a split second ahead of me. It was a blow out. It was devastating. I was totally demoralized. He won by a decision. I don't know how he didn't pin me. I had never had a match like that, even against world champs."

Uetake was born in Japan. But he was also made in the USA. He was a part of that limited but growing number of young people who traveled to distant and unknown lands to learn and grow. In the case of the twenty-year-old, a national high school wrestling champion in his home-

---

29   Harald Lechenperg, *Olympic Games 1964 Innsbruck Tokyo* (A.S. Barnes and Co.), 297.

town of Oura, Gunma, Uetake's journey would take him through Stillwater, Oklahoma.

While teenage Uetake was dreaming of going to the 1964 Tokyo Olympics, the commissioner of the Japanese Wrestling Federation, Ichiro Hatta, was working on fulfilling a promise to Myron Roderick, American Olympian at the Melbourne Games in 1956, and head coach of the Oklahoma State University wrestling team that would dominate NCAA wrestling in the United States throughout the remainder of the twentieth century.

Hatta had previously sent a strong Japanese wrestler to the United States in order to compete for Roderick at OSU, but that wrestler peeled off to Brigham Young University instead. According to the OSU sports magazine, *Posse*, "It made Mr. Hatta mad and he told Myron not to worry, that he would send him a better wrestler; that's when Yojiro showed up."[30]

Yojiro, or Yojo, as Americans called him, moved to the US reluctantly. After all, he couldn't speak English. But at least Stillwater, Oklahoma, had the small-town feel he was familiar with in Gunma—people were friendly. And he liked the food, particularly hamburger steaks and gravy, fried chicken, and ice cream!

---

30   Gene Johnson, "Discipline, Sacrifice, Concentration," *Posse*, 8 (Spring 2015).

Fortunately, Uetake knew how to control his weight so he could compete for the Oklahoma State University Cowboys. And compete he did, like no other Cowboy in its hallowed history. Yojiro Uetake never lost a match, winning three straight individual Big 8 and NCAA wrestling championships from 1963-1965, going an incredible 58-0 in collegiate competition.

What was the secret to his success?

Uetake had a great relationship with his coach, Myron Roderick. "He was a very strong wrestler," Uetake said. "He was passionate, strong in fundamentals and technique, and I really liked his focus on getting take downs. 'Take 'em down and let 'em go,' he would say about how to get two points quickly." The admiration was mutual. According to Roderick's wife, Jo Ann, "Myron always said that Yojiro had natural talent, and was by far the best wrestler he ever saw or coached."[31]

Uetake also had a great relationship with the OSU football team, taking health and physical education courses with them, including future Dallas Cowboys star fullback, Walt Garrison. "He was one of the greatest athletes I ever saw," Garrison said. And apparently Garrison and his teammates saw a lot of Uetake, because the football coach not only allowed him into the practices, he allowed

---

31   Gene Johnson, "Discipline, Sacrifice, Concentration."

him to practice with them. Uetake credits football training, like running inside ropes, hitting tackling dummies in quick succession, moving side to side, and fast-paced push-ups and sit-ups, for helping him hone his technique. "Tackling from a squat is great for wrestling as we are in the same stance, where we need to be ready to attack, hit, and get back, and get ready again," Uetake said.

Living in America had a profound effect on the young wrestler. Not only was he coached by Roderick and taken under the wing of the OSU football team, he learned how to build his own style of training. At the time, the NCAA did not allow coaches to train their wrestlers during the summer season. Instead, Uetake, who had to work to supplement his meager funds, would go to the Delta and Grand Junction in the Colorado mountains, which was like a desert, for work. And to keep in shape, he'd come up with ways to train. Uetake said he would have to lift very heavy bales of hay, but he'd do it in a way to work on specific muscles. He also maintained his feel for combat by actually tackling trees.

If he was in Japan, Uetake said, he would be wrestling all the time, and following the directions of his coach. And he would never have developed his own way of training or learned how to best take advantage of his own body and physical gifts. "I did this myself," he said. "Roderick taught me how to focus, but I learned a lot on my own."

All of that training, all of that innovation, finally came into play in the final three minutes of the gold medal match between Uetake and Akbas. Down 0-1, Uetake wanted to go for Akbas's leg, but the Turk was matching Uetake's moves and shifts. With only two minutes and forty seconds remaining, Uetake's instincts took over. He could not remember what happened next, except that he used his speed and guile to grab Akbas's leg and bring him down to the mat.

Two points.

Gold medal.

Tossed into the air by his teammates, Uetake was no longer an unknown. He was an Olympic hero—on two continents.

THE START OF THE PARALYMPIC MOVEMENT IN ASIA

Very few Japanese athletes, or Japanese citizens for that matter, had the opportunity Uetake did: go overseas, learn how to be independent, and understand that there are other ways, sometimes better ways, to achieve the same goals.

That was the power of the 1964 Olympiad—an opportunity for the world to come to Japan, for Japanese to see what world-class sports performance looked like, and what the very best did to be the best. And while the Olympic athletes inspired young men and women in Japan to dream, it was the Paralympic athletes of 1964 who arguably had a bigger impact, inspiring disabled men and women in Japan to live their lives more fully.

Incredibly, in contrast to the five years of planning and organizing devoted to the Tokyo Olympics, the Tokyo Paralympics came together quite suddenly, with an official organization to plan and execute the games established only sixteen months before the event. While the Paralympics and Olympics are a joint deal for host cities today, that was not the case in the 1960s. In his paper, *Tokyo's Other Games*, Dennis J. Frost of Kalamazoo College wrote that when the first Paralympics were held after the Rome Olympics in 1960, "a mere handful of people in Japan were aware of their existence."[32]

In other words, the idea of organizing an international competition for disabled athletes prior to 1962 was essentially nonexistent. Frost tells the incredible story of how very quickly a small group of people established new organizations, created public awareness, built consensus among local and national leaders, raised funds, and then actually ran the event. If not for a housewife,

---

32 Dennis J. Frost, "Tokyo's Other Games: The Origins and Impact of the 1964 Paralympics," *The International Journal of the History of Sport* 4 (March, 2012): 619-637.

a couple of impassioned bureaucrats, and a doctor in far-off Kyushu, there would likely have been no Tokyo Paralympics in 1964.

Hanako Watanabe was the wife of the Rome bureau chief of the Kyodo News Agency, and she attended the second-ever Paralympics, then called the Stoke Mandeville Games, named after the hospital where the first such games occurred at the same time as the 1948 London Olympics. Japan had no participants at the Rome Paralympics. But Watanabe did have an academic background in labor and welfare policy, and, more importantly, she had met the father of the Paralympic movement, Ludwig Guttmann. It is said the two met and talked about the possibility of holding a similar event in Japan after the Tokyo Olympics.

Watanabe gave talks and met with various government and non-government offices related to aiding the disabled. She also introduced her Japanese contacts to Guttmann. But in terms of concrete progress for the disabled, little progressed.

Arguably the key figure in bringing the Paralympics to Japan was Dr. Yutaka Nakamura, who lived in Oita, Kyushu, in Western Japan. Nakamura, and a local government official, Atsushi Hirata, organized Japan's first competition for disabled athletes on October 22, 1961.

Their success, while not highly publicized, became the model for a practical application for the thinkers in Tokyo.

Now that people in Japan could see what a Tokyo Paralympics might look like, supporters began to emerge. Susumu Iimuro, a leader of a large volunteer service organization called Lions Club International, joined hands with Muneyoshi Terada, an official of the Asahi Shimbun Social Welfare Organization, to announce their "across-the-board support" for steps leading to Japan's hosting of the next Stoke Mandeville Games. Terada then led the creation of a concrete plan to bring the Paralympics to Japan, the establishment of a preparatory committee, and then a series of consensus-building meetings with relevant officials in the Health and Welfare Ministry.

With momentum building, the movement got a monumental boost in August of 1962. Of all the acts and decisions made toward creating awareness about the disabled in society and the impact sports can have on the health of disabled athletes, one of the strategically important ones was involving the Crown Prince of Japan, Akihito, and his wife, the Crown Princess, Michiko. The fairy tale of a commoner meeting the Crown Prince on a tennis court, leading to a 1959 royal wedding covered feverishly by the media, was still strong in the hearts of the Japanese. So when the Crown Prince met with members of the Preparatory Committee, and stated afterwards that he hoped that the Paralympics would become a reality in Tokyo in 1964, media coverage and favorable public attitudes toward the Paralympics grew. Riding the wave of support, Prime Minister Hayato Ikeda pledged government assistance.

By May of 1963, it was official. The Health and Welfare Ministry approved the incorporation of a newly formed committee, the Organizing Committee for the Paralympic Games, in April, and a few weeks later, on May 13, a letter was sent to Guttmann and his fellow Stoke Mandeville committee members informing them of their intent to host the 1964 Stoke Mandeville Games in Tokyo after the Tokyo Olympics.

At that stage, despite the late hour, Japan's famed organizing efficiency took over, with every care taken to ensure that the event would occur flawlessly.

Crown Prince Akihito and Princess Michiko, courtesy of PHOTO KISHIMOTO

"MY SPIRIT LIFTED HIGH"

Only two weeks after the exhilarating Tokyo Olympiad, the 1964 Tokyo Paralympics, which ran from November 8 to 12, created an entirely new set of images and impressions on the Japanese psyche regarding notions of what disabled people could do.

Hundreds of foreign Paralympians were in Japan, serving as role models in terms of performance and attitude. According to Kazuo Ogoura, in his paper, *The Legacy of the 1964 Tokyo Paralympics*, their presence and their bearing were a jolt to Japanese society, which had until then tended to shun people with disabilities. As an administrator of the Paralympic Village put it, according to Ogoura, he remembers his surprise at seeing foreigners with disabilities so happy and full of life.

We were stunned to see overseas athletes in wheelchairs, hanging onto the back of a slow-operating Athlete Village loop bus to hitch a ride. It was sheer astonishment to witness their energy, enjoying themselves at a dance party at the International Club, or catching a taxi at night and loading their wheelchairs as well to go to Shibuya's entertainment precinct.[33]

The Japanese athletes who were asked to participate in the 1964 Paralympics likely had very little time to prepare, as the institutionalization of sports for disabled people had only just begun in Japan in the early 1960s. But when placed in a situation that tested their skills on an international platform, Japanese participants felt a rush of elation at being asked to stretch and compete.

A Japanese fencer, Shigeo Aono, felt empowered by the Paralympics in Japan, in a life-changing way.

Some said we were out of our minds for trying to compete in fencing, a traditional western sport, after just eight months of practice. Yet, we rejected the naysayers, followed through with our intentions and managed to win the silver medal—which gave us a powerful realization that we could do anything if we tried. That sense of confidence

---

33   Kazuo Ogoura, "The Legacy of the 1964 Tokyo Paralympics," *Journal of the Nippon Foundation Paralympic Research Group* 1 (January, 2015, 28).

gave me strong insight and courage, which has been a guiding force of my life ever since.[34]

Japanese discus thrower, Masayoshi Koike, said it more succinctly, "I had so much fun, with my spirit lifted high into the sky."

With confidence came the realization for Japanese athletes that they were not disabled, but enabled. They took heart in seeing how independent the foreign athletes in Tokyo were, refusing assistance from officials and getting around on their own far more than the average disabled Japanese. They also learned that part of being more independent was being more accountable to one's own health and condition.

Another demonstration of overseas athletes' independent mindset was the day-to-day effort that went into boosting their physical strength and athletic abilities. Japanese athletes were reminded of the importance of maintaining and increasing physical strength in daily life, when they witnessed the large number of injuries sustained by their teammates during the Paralympics. Two Japanese athletes suffered Achilles tendon injuries and fourteen others sustained a range of other injuries during their respective events.

---

34   Kazuo Ogouro, "The Legacy," 25.

The common attitude was to treat anyone with a disability with kid gloves, as people who needed constant care and careful handling. But at the 1964 Tokyo Paralympics, spectators and television viewers saw that the participants were athletes, not victims. Ogoura highlights this example of one of the swimmers:

> One female athlete from overseas had to be carried by her husband to get into the swimming pool. When the race started, she was left behind the rest straight away. By the time the first swimmer finished the race, she had only just swum about five meters. She would start sinking, but get back afloat. Rescue staff was swimming about two meters behind her just in case. When she began sinking after so many times, the rescue staff proceeded to help, but her husband on the poolside used a hand gesture to tell them to stop. Two more meters to go...one more meter...the progress was slow. Applause broke out in the spectators' stand. After more than three minutes, she finally completed the 25-meter feat. Episodes like this prompted eminent persons and sporting officials to express the opinion that "Disabled sports must be fostered as regular athletic events."[35]

Thanks to these examples, the government also awakened to the possibilities. Seiichiro Ide of the Ministry of Health and Welfare, acknowledging that "Japan had the culture of shunning people with disabilities," asserted

---

35 Kazuo Ogouro, "The Legacy," 27-28.

that from then on, "making the disabled more visible in society" was a new goal for the new Japan.

Another significant effect of the 1964 Tokyo Paralympics was the shift in the medical world, where doctors and institutions began to realize the need to focus more on rehabilitation, not just cure or prevention of disease; that to ignore the state of the disabled, who may have the potential of athletes seen at the 1964 Paralympics, is to ignore the opportunity to bring confidence and joy to a significant part of the population. Ogoura quotes a healthcare worker:

> Modern medicine focused too much on diseases and ignored people who suffer from them. It was the case of hunters being too busy looking for deer to look at the mountain itself, as they say in Japanese. Take spinal cord injuries for example. If medicine had focused more on achieving patients' recovery than merely treating the condition, I have no doubt that those with spinal cord injuries today would have enjoyed a higher level of physical recovery, even joining in on the funfair of the Paralympics.

The exposure to foreign equipment used by the disabled was also hugely impactful. When the hundreds of foreign Paralympians, coaches, and administrators came to Tokyo in 1964, they brought things that Japanese people had never seen, and immediately set the standard for Japan. Ogoura cited wheelchairs:

The greatest technological impact the Paralympics had was on the development and proliferation of equipment and tools for the care of those with disabilities, which were still underdeveloped in Japan at the time. There was a clear performance gap between foreign-made and Japanese wheelchairs and urine collectors, etc. Commenting on this matter, Yutaka Nakamura said, "The difference of wheelchairs was as clear as day." British sport-use wheelchairs weighed 13 kilograms, whereas Japanese wheelchairs were as heavy as 23 kilograms. Overseas players had wheelchairs made to suit their physique, while Japanese sport wheelchairs were the case of one-size-fits-all.

The Japanese could see the difference in performance based on the foreign athletes' use of the wheelchairs compared to themselves. Said one athlete, "Overseas players are bigger, but very skilled at handling their wheelchairs. We looked more like the wheelchairs were handling us. Then again, the experience gave us confidence that practice would improve our skills."

The 1964 Tokyo Paralympics caused a monumental mind shift in Japanese society. Dr. Yutaka Nakamura, one of the key players in making the Tokyo Paralympics happen, wrote in 1964 something that is the essential message of inclusion today:

Our society in general tends to underestimate the capability of people with disabilities. An event like this is significant in that it is a wonderful opportunity to demonstrate their capability to the rest of the society.

ANN PACKER AND THE JAPANESE SURPRISING THE WORLD

The same could be said, at the time, for women, who were under-represented at the 1964 Tokyo Olympics. While the 2020 Tokyo Games will come close to reaching an overall ratio of 50:50 men and women participants, women represented only 13 percent (or 678) of the total 5,151 people invited to the 1964 Tokyo Games.

Ann Packer was a 400-meter sprinter who was narrowly beaten by Australian Betty Cuthbert in the 400-meter finals. She was happy with her silver medal and ready to enjoy carefree moments shopping in the Ginza. As far as she was concerned, her Olympiad was over. Her fiancé and captain of the British athletics team, Robbie Brightwell, was astounded about how casual Ann was, and explained in his autobiography that she had a chance at history if she could hold off the urge to shop.[36]

36   Robbie Brightwell, Robbie Brightwell and his Golden Girl: The Posh and Becks of Yesteryear (Robbie Brightwell, 2011), ebook location 3772.

"Do you think I should run in the 800-meter heats tomorrow?" she asked. "Maybe I should call it a day and go shopping."

I gaped in astonishment. "Shopping? You must be mad! Shopping? This is the Olympic games, not the Moulsford Village sports!"

"I know, but I'm hardly likely to better a silver medal, am I? And I need to buy some presents for the folks back home."

"Come off it!" I exploded. "Think about the British girls back home who would have given their eyeteeth to be here in your place!"

She smiled sheepishly. "OK I'll run. Not that it'll make much difference. I'm bound to get eliminated in the heats, and then I can go shopping."

As it turns out, Packer and perhaps even her fiancé Brightwell were missing the telltale signs of potential success. While Packer hoped just to remain respectable, others saw a form and ease that would translate easily to victory. As Packer prepared for the finals, after essentially just making the cuts in the heats, two people of considerable experience and respect came up to Packer with powerfully motivating words. Again, here is how Brightwell explains it in his autobiography:

Milkha Singh jogged past with his 1,600-meter relay squad. Espying her, he dashed over, taking both hands and staring stern-faced into her eyes. "Ann Packer, listen to me. You will win!" She giggled self-conscientiously, flashing me an amused smile. Shaking her hands emphatically, he repeated his message.

"You're not listening, Ann Packer! Yesterday, I watched your semi-final. You were coasting! After the race, you come and show me your gold medal."

She nodded respectfully. No sooner he departed than Percy Cerutty, Betty Cuthbert's coach, rushed up. Even though they had never been introduced, Percy wasn't a man for social ceremonies. "This," he said, wagging a finger in front of her face, "is the finger of experience. And it's standing to attention. Listen! Betty and I've been talking. Stay with them until the end, and you will hammer them. Understand?"

Astonished, Ann nodded dumbly. Mission completed, Percy disappeared as quickly as he'd appeared.[37]

When Packer won her race, right away she steered to the stands and into the arms of Brightwell. Milkha Singh was there as well, smiling with the satisfaction of clairvoyance proved correct. "Did I not say your woman would win?

37   Robbie Brightwell, *Robbie Brightwell and his Golden Girl* ,ebook location 3841.

You didn't believe me! I was right! Hee, hee, hee! Brightwell, you never listen to me!"[38]

Ann Packer and Robbie Brightwell, courtesy of PHOTO KISHIMOTO

38 Robbie Brightwell, *Robbie Brightwell and his Golden Girl*, ebook location 3950.

Packer had little experience in the 800 meters. But that was true for all the other competitors. For the first half of the twentieth century, the IOC believed they were protecting women from competing in what they believed to be overly strenuous competitions for the fair sex. Thus, after 1928, women didn't run as far as 800 meters in the Olympics until 1960.

As a result, very few women were experienced at this distance. Packer had no preconceptions about how to run the race. But being naïve, and being a sprinter, was Packer's advantage. Packer was at the back of the pack for most of the race. But in the final 200 meters, she climbed to third, and in a burst sprinted out a dominating finish. A world record finish, in fact. As she later said, "Ignorance proved to be bliss."

Japan, as an emerging economy in 1964, was similar to Packer in the 800. Any new goal was a new challenge without any preconceptions about how to get things done. If they had a problem to solve, they tried anything and everything, leveraging what resources were available and learning from the world.

Toyota's famed just-in-time (JIT) lean manufacturing methodology has been recognized the world over as a superior process to maximize both quality and efficiency, leading to the transformation of the auto industry by the Japanese. Instead of stocking large inventories of doors that sat in a warehouse unused for weeks and exposed to potential damage, as was the case with large American manufacturers in Detroit, the Japanese engineers improvised.

With little capital available during those lean postwar years, they could not "waste" money on one or two months of stock. So parts were built only when they were going to be used—just in time. Capital was used efficiently, parts were not damaged while sitting for weeks, and everyone on an assembly line was charged with the mandate to innovate in any way that eliminated waste and improved quality.

And so, even in 1964, to the surprise of visiting Olympians, Japanese products were not cheap and low quality. They were cutting edge.

Packer and Brightwell flew to Tokyo with their fellow Olympians on British Overseas Airways Comet, the world's first commercial jet airliner. They had the opportunity to visit the cockpit and talk with the pilot. They asked about Japan, and Brightwell asked the well-traveled pilot whether he had any recommendations for things to buy there.

He said, "Yeah, Seiko watches. They make fantastic watches. Get a movie camera. Get a tape recorder. You got to get one of those transistor radios. And a camera. Oh, I see you're wearing glasses. Go and get contact lenses." So I did see the optician one day in Tokyo. And got them the next day! The Japanese were already making gas-permeable contact lenses. They were brilliant. For my first race, I could actually see the track.

We were very impressed. We knew about Japanese engineering in heavy industry, but we didn't know anything about their use of American transistors and computers in Japan. We could see they were moving to higher-value, technologically intense products.

Brightwell was friendly with members of the British press, including BBC sports star commentator and presenter, David Coleman. Brightwell said that his conversations with Coleman in Tokyo were often about how many things he had learned about the innovative way Japan was televising the Games—that these Games would be the first to be globally broadcast by satellite; that there were dozens of movie cameras in the National Stadium, when the BBC might employ two; that the media in the Press section had events results provided to them by computers; that the Games were going to be seen in color in many homes in Japan, while most in England had to settle for black and white.

"Relatively speaking," said Brightwell, "we were still on steam locomotives."

SEIKO—SEIZING THE MOMENT, MAKING A DIFFERENCE

In 1959, when Tokyo was awarded the XVIII Olympiad by the IOC, Seiko's President, Shoji Hattori, was determined to make Seiko the official timer of the Olympic Games. In 1960, he sent a telegram to one of his watch design section managers, Saburo Inoue, with instructions that would forever change the fate of the Japanese watch company—"Intend to handle official timing duties. Go to Rome Olympics in August and observe timing procedures."[39]

Inoue was deeply skeptical of the idea, and for good reason. "I'd never seen timing devices for the Olympics," he said. "I didn't know how they used their stopwatches, or what types they would need. We couldn't do computer simulations, so we had to work out every single thing by trial and error."

But again, as explained in the 2012 *The Daily Telegraph* article, ignorance proved to be bliss.

In those days, it was the prerogative of the local organizing committee to select the company that would supply

---

39   Tracey Llewellyn, "When Olympic Clocks Almost Stopped," *The Daily Telegraph*, May, 26, 2012.

the timers, and it was likely they would choose the tried-and-true Swiss watchmakers—Omega or Longines. Up till then, they were the only firms trusted with ensuring accurate times in Olympic competition.

In contrast, Seiko's experience in building timers specifically for sports was zero. Such was the confidence of Hattori and Japan at the time—that anything was possible if they tried.

Without assurance of a contract for the Olympics, Hattori asked his three group companies to work on Olympic-related projects: large clocks, stopwatches, crystal chronometers, and a new idea, a device that could print the times of competitors right after the end of a race. They were called printing timers, and this revolutionized the way results of competitions were determined.

In only two years, Seiko was producing sports stopwatches that passed the standards of the International Association of Athletics Federations (IAAF) Technical Committee. In a track and field competition in Belgrade, Yugoslavia, the IAAF was witness to a successful test, as the Japanese-made stopwatches proved accurate and reliable.

Seiko had already successfully developed quartz technology for small watches, and used this crystal technology for long distance races, like the marathon among others.

Developing this quartz technology was key to developing Seiko wristwatches of the future that would stay accurate over longer periods of time.

More significantly, perhaps for the athletes, was Seiko's development of the printing timer, a machine that would electronically time and print the results of an event, up to 1/100 of a second for track events.

This machine had a significant impact on a high-visibility competition at the 1964 Tokyo Olympics—the women's 80-meter hurdles final.

On October 19, at the National Stadium, Karin Balzer of Germany and Teresa Cieply of Poland settled into their starting blocks. When the pistol shot rang, an electric signal was sent via wire to a printing timer, as well as a signal to a camera that would take special photo finish pictures, and a signal to a large spectator clock that set the second-hand in motion.[40]

In a stunning finish, Balzer, Cieply, and Australian Pam Kilborn hit the tape seemingly in a dead heat, all three timed by officials at 10.5 seconds. Despite numerous officials with hand stopwatches that measured in tenths of seconds, officials could not determine a winner.

---

40   International Olympic Committee, Games of the XVIII Olympiad Tokyo 1964—The Official Report of the Organizing Committee, (1964), 177-8.

The officials preferred not to hand out three gold medals, and fortunately, had a fallback plan—the latest timing technology from Japan.

When the runners arrived at the goal, a picture was taken by a slit camera, manufactured by Japan Photo Finish Co. Ltd. After thirty seconds, the image's negative was transmitted as a reflected image, and converted in three minutes to a positive print. The information from Seiko's printing timer was integrated into an image noting times in hundredths of seconds. The photo would show not only the athletes, but time, and thus the order in which they finished.

Thanks to the printing timer, it was revealed that Balzer completed the race in 10.54 seconds, 0.01 seconds ahead of Cieply, who was also only 0.01 seconds ahead of Kilborn. While the IAAF officially recognized times to the tenth of a second, in this case, they accepted the recorded electronic time to the hundredth.

The printing timer contributed mightily to the evolution of timed sports, and led to the creation of the famed, global printing company—EPSON—its name a simple mash-up of the words "son of electronic printer."

1964 was Seiko's time.

1964 was Japan's time.

CHAPTER 4

STANDING UP AND PUSHING BACK

RIKIDOZAN, GODZILLA, AND THE ATOMIC BOMB BOY

DAWN FRASER AND THE INFAMOUS FLAG INCIDENT OF 1964

Dawn Fraser was on top of the world after winning gold and silver medals, contributing to her total haul of eight medals over three Olympiads. She was honored with the task of carrying the Australian flag in the closing ceremony on Saturday, October 24, 1964.

But it was Friday, and the night was still young. And when you're Dawn Fraser, you can't help but let a bit of the larrikin out.

The competitions were over, and the party was on at the Imperial Hotel. The Australian swim team had gone home already, but Fraser had the entire Australian hockey team to party with. As she described in her book, *Dawn: One Hell of a Life*, "at one stage our interpreter gave her kimono to Lee Robinson (director of a film crew following Fraser) while she wore my bathrobe, which was several sizes too big for her, and they danced about in their ridiculous outfits."

Around 2:30 a.m., a little less than twelve hours prior to when Fraser was scheduled to march into the National Olympic Stadium carrying her country's flag, a plan was being hatched. An official on the Australian team, Dr. Howard Toyne, suggested that they embark on a shady tradition of sorts in the Olympics—pinching flags—and that he knew just the place to find them. One of the hockey players, Des Piper, overheard the plotting and joined the adventure.

The three partners in crime slipped away from the party and walked through the darkened Tokyo streets until they arrived at the Emperor's Palace, where they saw the white flags of the Olympic rings surrounding the place, spaced fifty feet apart.

> We decided we wanted a flag each, and Howard and I held Des up on our shoulders because Des was the smallest.

They were quite easy to get loose and we had two down and were going for the third flag when whistles started sounding.[41]

They ran up a hill and hid behind bushes, but when the police began literally beating the bushes with their nightsticks, Toyne and Piper peeled off. Fraser thought it best to stay hidden while their pursuers all went running after her friends, her flag safely tucked under her tracksuit jacket.

After about ten minutes I decided I'd make a break for it and jumped down from the wall that ran across the top of the rise where I'd been hiding. My ankle twisted under me as I landed, but I ignored the pain and ran on toward a low hedge, about three feet tall. I went to jump over the hedge, not realizing it had barbed wire as I desperately tried to untangle myself and jump down on the other side. Unfortunately, this time I landed in a pond and found myself waist-deep in cold, murky water. I stayed very quietly in the pond for another fifteen minutes. It began to get very cold and the pond was a bit smelly.[42]

She climbed out of the water, and thinking she was now safe and sound, she sat on a park bench to rest and consider her next step, when two policemen came upon her.

41 Dawn Fraser, *Dawn: One Hell of a Life* (Hodder, 2001), 193.

42 Dawn Fraser, Dawn: One Hell of a Life, 194.

When they noticed the rope of the flag peeking out of her tracksuit, they pulled on it and the flag came tumbling out.

As the policemen began to lead Fraser away, she saw a bicycle, which one of the policemen had come on.

> I shouted really loudly, "There are my friends over there!" And when they looked I ran forward, grabbed the bike and started pedaling like crazy. All of a sudden police came from every direction blowing their whistles again and I was forced to get off the bike and go with them down past the Imperial Palace Hotel to the Marunouchi police station on the corner.[43]

At the police station, no one would believe that she was an Olympic athlete, let alone the world-famous Dawn Fraser. She had no identification on her, so the best she could do in the middle of the night was to contact a friend to bring her identification and vouch for her. This friend was Lee Robinson, the director. He brought the ID, and the police were finally convinced that she was who she said she was. Robinson also urged that she needed to be on her way so she could march at the head of the Australian squad at the closing ceremony, and that wouldn't it be a good idea to, you know, keep this hush-hush?

---

43   Dawn Fraser, Dawn: One Hell of a Life, 195.

Dawn Fraser, courtesy of PHOTO KISHIMOTO

The police captain did indeed agree, and some ten hours later Fraser, visibly limping for some unknown reason, held the Australian flag aloft in front of 75,000 people.

The business of the police captain was not yet finished, however. During the Closing Ceremony, he paid a visit and delivered a box with a present inside.

It was the stolen Olympic flag!

THE SECURITY TREATY CRISIS OF 1960

Fraser's theft was seen by the authorities as a playful act; in the end, they felt, it was more important to provide comfort and joy to the foreign visitor, particularly such an honored guest as the Australian swimming legend, than to stand on the letter of the law.

This welcoming and flexible attitude touched athletes and visitors alike, who were unanimous in their praise of Japanese friendliness, cleanliness, efficiency, and effectiveness. The foreigners were cheerfully buying up cameras and radios, while the Japanese themselves were filling their homes with televisions, refrigerators, and washing machines.

The head of the International Olympic Committee, Avery Brundage, not one known for his warm and fuzzy style, joined in the acclamation, citing one of the more "callous" journalists he knew who labeled the Tokyo Olympics the "Happy Games."

The popular songs of the time reflect the upbeat attitudes of the era. Visiting athletes would have heard the syrupy melody of the international hit, "Sukiyaki, which sold over 13 million records and amazingly made it to the Billboard Hot 100 charts in the United States in 1963, despite the fact that it was sung entirely in Japanese; as well as the bouncy tune, "Konnichi wa Akachan" ("Hello My Baby"), sung cheerfully by Michiyo Azusa. The call of the mother to her little baby in this song was a symbol of Japan's feeling of hope and optimism, akin to how a parent might feel about their child as they embark on the journey of life.

Konnichiwa, my baby and your beautiful smile

Konnichiwa, my baby and your precious cry

Your tiny hand, your round eyes

It's so nice to meet you, I'm your mama!

And yet, it was only four years earlier when societal and political forces seemingly threatened the continued momentum of democracy in Japan, as well as Japan's improving reputation around the world.

It was June 10, 1960, and James C. Hagerty, the Press Secretary for President Dwight D. Eisenhower, had flown into Haneda Airport in Tokyo, to finalize preparations for the first visit of an American president to Japan. The visit was scheduled for June 19, part of a goodwill exchange in which Crown Prince Akihito would also visit the United States to celebrate one hundred years of Japan and US relations.

When Hagerty's plane landed, an estimated 10,000 demonstrators were outside the airport, and many others filled the terminal building. Hagerty and Ambassador Douglas MacArthur II got into a limousine and went through a tunnel, which opened onto a bridge where hundreds of students and workers were massing in the hope of disrupting Hagerty's arrival. At issue was the extension of the Security Treaty that bound the two countries together. According to the book by George R. Packard, *Protest in Tokyo*, Hagerty had a scare.

> When the car stopped, the disorganized crowd mauled it badly, cracking windows, denting fenders, and rocking it back and forth; several leaders jumped onto the roof and led the singing of the "Internationale" and the chanting of "Hagachi Go Homu!" and "Don't Come Aiku!" No one tried to open the door or attack Hagerty, but at one time both right wheels were lifted off the ground.[44]

Eisenhower did indeed cancel his trip to Japan. And

44 George R. Packard, *Protest in Tokyo: The Security Treaty Crisis of 1960* (Princeton University Press, 1966), 289-90.

the so-called Hagerty Incident was one of many that reflected the prevailing Cold War tensions, as well as the ambivalent attitude of the Japanese toward their American overlords, and the Security Treaty that defined their relationship.

The first Security Treaty was signed in 1951, at a time when the United States was readying Japan for the end of the Occupation, while still allowing for the continued presence of US bases and troops. The Security Treaty was signed hard upon the signing of the peace treaty between the two countries. George Packard, who is currently president of the United States-Japan Foundation and who was present in Tokyo in 1960, explained that the Japanese had little choice in the matter.

> The peace treaty was welcomed, to be sure, as a first step in liquidating the costly and humiliating defeat. The security treaty, clearly a condition of the peace treaty, was accepted with resignation and the belief that it could not be avoided. There was the feeling that Japan was in no position to insist on the removal of the very forces which were "giving" her the peace treaty.[45]

In 1959, the IOC felt it was now time to bring the Olympics to Asia, and awarded the 1964 Games to Tokyo. Japan

---

45   George R. Packard, *Protest in Tokyo: The Security Treaty Crisis of 1960* (Princeton University Press, 1966), 11.

was getting back on its feet economically, and a growing number of Japanese were wondering how much longer American soldiers had to stay in their country.

There was a perceptible anti-American sentiment. When Gary Powers's U-2 plane was shot down over Soviet air space in May 1960, the Japanese wondered if the plane had taken off from Japanese soil. It had actually taken off from an airfield in Pakistan, but the Japanese were sensitive to the so-called "black jets" because one had made an emergency landing near Fujisawa in Japan, which was of course not known until the Japanese press uncovered the story. The November 28, 1959, Mainichi Shimbun editorial expressed the concern of the time: "We begin to wonder in whose hands Japan's sovereignty really lies... In fact, we are still subordinate."

On June 20, 1960, the House of Councilors passed the bill revising domestic laws to allow Japan to ratify the Treaty of Mutual Cooperation and Security with the United States, thus ending a period of countless demonstrations and political unrest. America was allowed to maintain its military presence in Japan, a signal to other nations that the United States would continue to work to thwart communist expansion in the region.

At the same time, Japan was now able to focus its efforts on its economy without having to shoulder the heavy expense of an independent military. Out went the highly unpopular prime minister, Nobusuke Kishi (formerly charged as a war criminal but released in return for his cooperation with Occupation authorities), and in came the energetic Hayato Ikeda, whose man-of-the-people image, as well as his focus on the burgeoning Japanese economy, won the favor of the public.

The protests against the Japanese and American governments stopped. But the Japanese had experienced what it was like to push back against authority. And while they realized that there were limits to how much disruption to harmonious relations they could cause, they also realized that the limits were farther out than they had believed. The lessons were applied later in the sixties when student rebellions closed down some of the country's leading universities.

Going back to the 1950s, after years of subordination to the American government, pop culture in Japan was already providing opportunities for the Japanese to visualize a more 'subversive' way to think.

RIKIDOZAN—A JAPANESE HERO RISES

It was Sunday, February 21, 1954. Thousands filled Kurumae Kokugikan, thousands more stood in front of large TV screens on various street corners, and millions sat in their homes to watch a professional wrestling match. This was the finale of a three-day wrestling tournament that featured two Japanese, Rikidozan, a former sumo wrestler, and Masahiko Kimura, a former judoka; and two brothers from America, Ben and "Iron Mike" Sharpe.

On Friday, February 19, the Japanese pair wrestled the Sharpes to a draw in a tag-team competition that lasted an hour. On Saturday, February 20, the format switched to individual competitions, where Iron Mike defeated Japanese wrestler Toshio Yamaguchi, and Rikidozan triumphed over Ben. So on Sunday, from 3:00 in the afternoon, wrestling was the only thing on the minds of Japanese across the country.

And as one might suspect, the third day ended in a tie— Mike defeating Kimura, Rikidozan defeating Mike, and the tag-team finale ending in what is called a "double count out." By virtue of the fact that the Sharpe brothers were already the champions, they were able to keep their title.

But that didn't matter to the Japanese. Rikidozan was significantly shorter and smaller than either of the Sharpe brothers—and yet he was able to take the taller and larger wrestlers down. The Sharpe brothers were the perfect foils to the Japanese hero who had to overcome his natural physical disadvantages and triumph with fair play and superior wrestling prowess.

Of course, Rikidozan and others in the wrestling game at the time understood that the creation of heroes and villains was a big part of the successful marketing of the sport. In Rikidozan's case, having a Japanese defeat an American in the ring was particularly good for business.

In the end, as Yoshikuni Igarashi eloquently explains in his book, *Bodies of Memory: Narratives of War in Postwar Japanese Culture, 1945-1970*, Rikidozan in his performance and orchestration of professional wrestling unified the Japanese like no other:

> Rikidozan's performance rehabilitated Japan's nationhood by casting Japan as a victor in the bloody fight against its adversary, the United States.[46]

It is now known that Rikidozan was actually of Korean origin and that the Sharpe brothers were Canadian. Nevertheless, to the Japanese, Rikidozan was their champion, their symbol of a powerful Japanese manhood that could stand proud and tall in the international arena and help bury the memories of the war years and the suffering that followed. The echoes of those same sentiments were all too evident when judoka Kaminaga faced off against Geesink, as described earlier, and go a long way to explain

---

46   Yoshikuni Igarashi, *Bodies of Memory: Narratives of War in Postwar Japanese Culture, 1945-1970* (Princeton, NJ: Princeton University Press, 1970), 125.

the depth of disappointment when the Japanese champion was taken down.

GODZILLA—HE WHO MUST NOT BE NAMED

Kids in America growing up in the 1970s and 1980s remember the poorly lip-synched but somehow lovable Godzilla films, featuring a rubber-suited protector of the human race against a legion of monsters bent on wreaking havoc on the earth, most particularly on the city of Tokyo. But the first Godzilla film in 1954, released only a few months after the Rikidozan-Sharpe brothers' showdown, was a dark tale with a serious message about the dangers of entry into the nuclear world. The black and white film also contained an interesting sub-context about Japan's attitude toward America.

According to Yoshikuni Igarashi, Godzilla was a reminder of the war's impact on Japan. When Japanese audiences watched Godzilla, a lizard-like monster emerging from the depths of the ocean and marching into Tokyo, flattening buildings and toppling towers, they again saw, in their minds' eye, the Tokyo devastated by American firebomb attacks only nine years earlier.

The film's producer, Tanaka Tomoyuki, saw Godzilla as an allegory for the awful destructive power that human beings faced in the nuclear age, disembodied from any specific geopolitical origin. Frustrated by the film's failure to indict American responsibility, however, one writer later insisted that Godzilla should have crossed the Pacific and attacked American cities, since the United States was responsible for the nuclear testing that created the monster in the first place.[47]

The opening scene of the film must have been a particularly visceral reminder to the Japanese of the horrors of war in the nuclear age. The crew of a Japanese fishing boat is relaxing after a hard day of work, when a flash of light appears across the water, and an explosion sets the boat on fire, and sinks it.

Only months before the film's release, on March 1, 1954, a tuna fishing boat named the Daigo Fukuryu-Maru was caught in the flaky-white fallout of an American hydrogen bomb test in the Bikini Atoll. All twenty-three crew members suffered acute radiation syndrome, with the crew's radioman succumbing six months later. This was a couple of years after the end of the Allied occupation and censorship, so the Japanese public was fully aware of the incident.

Japan in 1954 was on the upswing, buoyed by the economic windfall of the Korean War as the US military made billions of dollars of procurement orders to Japa-

---

47   Yoshikuni Igarashi, *Bodies of Memory*, 115.

nese manufacturers. Going to the theater to watch a film was a popular way for the rising middle class to enjoy a bit of leisure.

And yet, Godzilla, which undoubtedly provided pleasure and escapism for millions, was also a blatant symbol of the horrific impact of nuclear weaponry, and thus tapped deeply felt emotions of victimization and resentment toward a Voldemort-like entity, its name never uttered—the United States. As Igarashi explains:

> In 1954, the concerted attacks (against Godzilla) that the film portrays would have been possible only with the help of American forces. Nevertheless, the Japanese *Boetai* (Defense Forces) and *Kaijo Hoantai* (Maritime Security Forces) are solely responsible for the attacks against Godzilla. If the monstrous body of Godzilla indeed embodied American nuclear threats, it is only logical that the Japanese forces alone should attack. The American forces by definition could not. Thus, the United States returns as an enemy—albeit an unnamed one—through the figure of Godzilla, invoking memories of the war.[48]

"ATOMIC BOMB BOY" AND THE SUBTLEST OF ANTI-AMERICAN PROTESTS

Seventeen-year-old Dick Roth, winner of the individual

---

48   Yoshikuni Igarashi, *Bodies of Memory*, 116.

medley race at the 1964 Tokyo Olympics, was thirteen years old when he first traveled with the US swim team to Japan in 1960. He remembers being treated like a celebrity. Toward the end of his stay, the team went to Nikko, the beautiful resort town not far from Tokyo. And while walking about the woods with the team, he saw something he clearly remembers today.

> I wandered off on my own, which was a habit I have when I travel, skipping the handlers. I was walking back to the lodge and I came face to face with a group of eight to ten horribly disfigured children of my age, probably older. They were from Nagasaki and Hiroshima. Later I talked with one of my handlers and asked about them. He said they were also on a tour. The organizers were trying to keep us apart. I was shocked and horrified. To think anyone could do anything so barbaric. I know we dropped the bomb to shorten the war. But it's a visceral feeling I will never forget.

Back in Tokyo four years later, Roth also remembers the Opening Ceremonies when a sole torchbearer ran into the National Stadium. "The torchbearer came in and there was cheering and a kind of reverence. I don't know what to call it. The attention was locked on this individual. I was stunned by the switch in the crowd. He got to the top and turned around. It was like another one of those moments that defies description. When he stood there and held the torch high, I was stunned."

Roth was referring to Yoshinori Sakai, who was born in Hiroshima on August 6, 1945, the day an atomic bomb was dropped on his city. "When he reached the bottom of the stairs he didn't stop, just ran up the stairs in stride. He only paused at the top, turning to face the full stadium and the world. He then turned and lit the flame, causing an entire nation a collective moment of pride and sadness."

Torchbearer Yoshinori Sakai, courtesy of PHOTO KISHIMOTO

It was a bold move. For a country that was trying desperately to erase from its collective memory the horrors of World War II, the Olympic organizers risked offending the United States of America by reminding the world that Japan was the first and only country to be attacked by nuclear weapons.

In fact, prominent Japanophile and translator of such classics as *The Tale of Genji*, American Edwin Seidensticker, said that the selection of Sakai as the final torchbearer was not "incidental," and was "unpleasant to Americans."[49]

When G. D. Sondhi of India, a member of the International Olympic Committee who had just witnessed Sakai's torch lighting at the opening ceremonies, was asked to comment on Seidensticker's reaction, he replied, "He (Sakai) is good and I'm happy to see him do it so nicely. We must bring young people in the Olympics and let those old men just sit and help them." Sondhi went on to say that he did not think Sakai's selection to be political, and rather thought that Sakai represented "a big hope" for Japan, and that his was "the most touching of all Olympic ceremonies I ever saw."

Still, it's amazing that the organizers, on Japan's biggest day, consciously chose to highlight Hiroshima via Sakai— whom the press dubbed "Atomic Bomb Boy"[50]—a poke in the ribs of the United States.

SUKIYAKI—A SONG OF THE TIMES

The songs highlighted at the top of the chapter, "Kon-

---

49 Hisashi Uno, "Prof. Seidensticker's Charge On Sakai Proves 'Unpopular'," *The Mainichi Daily News*, October 11, 1964.

50 Robert Whiting, "Opening Ceremony Ushered in New Era for Japan," *The Japan Times*, October 14, 2014.

nichiwa Akachan" and "Sukiyaki" were both penned by the same lyricist, Rokusuke Ei, who revolutionized Japanese pop music with his phrasing.

His phrasing was simple, a change from the flowery lyrics of the 1950s, and yet in the case of the international hit, Sukiyaki, sung by popular crooner Kyu Sakamoto, the meaning of the lyrics has a level of complexity rooted in the times.

This was of course lost on the international crowd, who did not understand Japanese. The easy-listening melody of the song was apparently so catchy, that the British producer who first promoted the song overseas decided that changing the name of the song to a popular Japanese dish would be a more effective sell. The actual title of the song is "Ue o Mite Arukou." In English that would literally translate as "Let's Look Up as We Walk."

If you don't listen closely, you might think "Ue o Mite Arukou" is a syrupy song about unrequited love, along the lines of "Tears of a Clown," by Smokey Robinson, or "I Wish It Would Rain," by The Temptations.

Let's look up as we walk

So that the tears won't fall

Remembering those spring days

But we are all alone tonight.

The lyricist, Ei, was in his late twenties and he was active in the demonstrations of the late 1950s and 1960s, at the peak of the protests against the passage of the Treaty of Mutual Cooperation and Security between the United States and Japan. When the treaty was ratified by the Japanese government, Ei was one of tens of thousands who felt the air had been let out of the ballooning protests, and that nothing but sadness and resignation remained. It is said that he wrote "Ue o Mite Arukou" as a reflection of his sadness and resignation.

And yet, depending on how you hear it, the words also manage to convey a sense of optimism, of keeping one's chin up in difficult times.

Happiness lies beyond the clouds

Happiness lies up above the sky

Let's look up as we walk

So that the tears won't fall

Though the tears well up as we walk

For tonight we are alone

In a way, "Ue o Mite Arukou" captured the spirit of the times—a song about protest, sung in a sweet and syrupy way conveying hope—that sold millions of records to an eager youth culture searching for happiness in material wealth.

After all, 1964 was not about controversy. 1964 was about welcoming the world and celebrating a new Japan.

After the years of hard work their parents put in, scrimping and saving, the Japanese youth were leading the consumerism charge, taking *vacances* around the country, filling bowling alleys, baseball stadiums and movie theaters, and becoming slaves to fashion. In the midst of the boom, engineers and designers were fearless in their creativity, looking to build the biggest and fastest in the world. Businessmen were insatiable in seeking abroad the very best ideas and technology. And students appealed passionately to the youth of the world, in search of pen pals, and a genuine desire for meaningful connection across the seas.

1964 was a time when the Japanese felt anything was possible. And the 1964 Tokyo Olympics was the realization for all of them that they could accomplish whatever they set out to do.

In fact, it's hard to imagine the Tokyo Olympics having

the same searing impression on the Japanese psyche if it were held in another year. In 1955, when Rome won the bid for the 1960 Olympics, Tokyo actually received four votes from IOC members. But the Japanese economy was just getting off the ground, so the prospect of a successful Asian Olympics still seemed remote.

If Tokyo had been selected as the host city for 1968, it is unlikely that the event would have been labeled the "Last Innocent Games," as it commonly is. Times were a' changing and 1968 was one of the most unstable years of the twentieth century, with the assassinations of Martin Luther King Jr. and Bobby Kennedy, massive protests in France, and increasing angst over the Vietnam War.

Only weeks before the start of the 1968 Mexico City Olympics, the Mexican government ordered the suppression of anti-government protests, resulting in the death of hundreds. And during the Olympics, sprinters Tommie Smith and John Carlos brought race relations in America to the fore with their raised fists on the medal stand.

Japan was also feeling the effects of a global clash in values and generations. In 1964, the Beatles were the most popular entertainers in the world, Japan no exception. In 1966, when they visited Tokyo for the first time on a sold-out concert tour, they traveled and performed under very tight security. Right-wingers shouted for the

Beatles to go home, and not to "desecrate" the concert venue, the Nippon Budokan, built for the training and competition of Japanese martial arts.

In 1968, student protests came to a violent head against the Japanese government and its support of the United States' war with Vietnam. Clashes between students on the left and on the right, and between students and the police were bloody.

Happily, 1964 was just the right time, a time to greet the world with open arms, a time to eagerly learn from the best in the world, a time to walk looking up with head held high.

CHAPTER 5

WINNING ISN'T EVERYTHING, LOSING ISN'T NOTHING

TO BE AMONG GIANTS

It was September 1960. Electronics engineer, Makoto Kikuchi, arrived in San Francisco and stayed overnight in a motel. A powerful and constant sound that reverberated around his room kept him awake. But when he realized that it was the sound of cars speeding down a highway like rockets, unlike the sound of cars in Tokyo puttering their herky-jerky way through the bumpy roads, Kikuchi knew he was in a different world.

The engineer was twenty-three when the transistor was invented in 1948, and soon the idea of two metal wires in a piece of silicon became an obsession, and a pathway to the prestigious Ministry of International Trade and Industry. MITI, as this powerhouse ministry was called, sent Kikuchi to Boston, for an assignment at one of the great American engineering universities, the Massachusetts Institute of Technology (MIT). And despite his thirty-five years, he felt like a kid in a candy store.[51]

> My room was located in Building 10, directly under the famous dome that is MIT's symbol. Down the hall to the right was a conference chamber called the Busch Room, and every Thursday at 4:00 p.m. this room would become the setting for a seminar. The people in charge of these seminars—Dr. von Hippel, Dr. J. C. Slater and others—were all doyens of the scientific community, scientists I had known of in Japan through their textbooks and papers. The real Dr. von Hippel was much smaller than I had imagined, a man in whose blue eyes I felt an almost mystical sensibility.

> At MIT and other schools of its caliber, almost all the professors were like that, so much so that you found yourself bumping into Nobel Prize winners in the halls and toilets. It was a tremendous stimulus that left me feeling like my brain had been recharged.

---

51 Makoto Kikuchi, *Japanese Electronics: A Worm's Eye View of Its Evolution* (The Simul Press Inc., March 1983), 43.

Kikuchi would go on to learn under the tutelage of W. B. Shockley, who along with J. Bardeen and W. Brattain, created the transistor. In fact, it was Shockley who asked to meet Kikuchi, after reading one of the Japanese engineer's published papers. When he heard that the inventor of the transistor wanted to meet him, Kikuchi could not contain himself. "I could have a discussion with W. B. Shockley! For a person like me, still polishing my skills as a researcher, these were the happiest tidings imaginable."

Kikuchi would become the director of research for the famed Sony Corporation in 1974, which would rise in the 1970s and 1980s to become one of the most influential electronics and consumer goods companies in the world, with their transistor radios, their televisions, and of course, their Walkmans.

But in the 1960s, Sony and so many other Japanese companies were in learning mode. The Japanese government was stingy in making foreign currency available to private enterprise, wanting to make sure that their limited capital was used to the greatest advantage to the Japanese economy. Part of that strategy was sending the right bureaucrats and engineers overseas to learn from the best. In the case of Kikuchi, American researchers and businessmen were, on the whole, sympathetic to the eager Japanese, and open with their knowledge and intellectual property. And they could not envision Japan as an economic threat any time soon.

To Kikuchi's surprise, his mentor Shockley offered him a job at his new company in Palo Alto. Kikuchi surprised Shockley back, saying, "I feel a uniquely American kind of freshness in the scientific research going on in the United States. Someday after I return to Japan, I would like to create this same kind of atmosphere in my own research group. That is my dream."

According to Kikuchi, the giant of twentieth-century electronics smiled and replied, "I wonder when you'll wake up?"

Kikuchi was awake. He was on a mission to learn what he could in the United States, and then come home and raise the standard in Japan.

Such was the case for thousands of athletes in Japan for the 1964 Tokyo Olympics. They were there to learn and bring new standards, practices, and beliefs back to their countries.

THOSE WORDS ARE FOR ME

Over 5,100 athletes attended the 1964 Tokyo Olympics, and over 500 medals were distributed to those who finished first, second, or third. In other words, some 90 percent of all athletes, or about 4,600 Olympians went home without a gold, silver, or bronze medal.

Most of the people who marched into the jam-packed National Stadium on October 10, 1964, would not win, or even come close. Singaporean cyclist A. Hamid Supa'at was one of those who was happy to be in Tokyo, but was not expecting to win.

Hamid Supa'at (3rd from right) with members of the Malaysian cycling team in Hachioji, courtesy of Hamid Supa'at

As they marched, the words of Baron Pierre de Coubertin, founder of the modern Olympic movement, appeared on the screen of the National Stadium, as if they were meant just for the 90 percent:

> The most important thing in the Olympic Games is not to win but to take part. Just as the most important thing in life is not the triumph but the struggle.

"Oh my," thought Hamid. "Those words are for me."

In 1964, there were twenty new countries participating in the Tokyo Olympic Games. And the majority of those athletes, perhaps every single one of those athletes, had no illusion of taking home a medal. As Hamid said, he was there to "meet the best athletes of each nation and make friends." Like Kikuchi in the United States, many were in Japan to participate, to experience, to learn, and bring back the stories and the standards of the world's best.

Malaysia was participating for the first time, a newly formed federation that included Singapore, Sarawak, and North Borneo. Malaysia, of course, is a part of Southeast Asia, which means temperatures are high. As they say in that area, there are three seasons: hot, hotter and hottest. October in Malaysia is probably in the season "hotter," with temperatures routinely around 27-30°C (80–86°F).

Unfortunately, on the day of the 190-kilometer road race in the Western part of Tokyo, it was rainy and cold.

The new Malaysian Olympic squad had nine cyclists, including the Singaporean Hamid, a long-distance road racer. Hamid found the conditions very difficult. "My cheeks were red. My hands were very cold. And I could see smoke coming out of my mouth," he said. "My coach told me to stack newspapers under my shirt to keep me warm. I had never raced in that weather before. It was always hot, hot, hot for me."

Hamid was a spry nineteen-year-old, someone who had competed in long-distance road races many times. In fact, he had participated months before in the Tour of Malaysia, winning two stages and two time trials. But nothing prepared him for the cold. And the lack of experience in such conditions didn't help either.

> The Europeans were all up front, and most of the Asians were in the back. The roads were wet, so it was very slippery. In the first few kilometers, we were all in one big bundle as we entered the first climb, where the road was very narrow. A few cyclists crashed, so those in front sprang ahead, while the rest got stuck.

Hamid was fortunate that he did not fall, but he had to bide his time before he could pick up any speed behind the crowd. He said he remembered everyone talking in many different languages about how they were stuck and couldn't do anything. In the end, the cold, wet weather took its toll on about 25 of the 132 cyclists, who failed to complete the 190-kilometer course. Hamid lasted only about half the race before he bowed out.

But he said it was a great experience as he had a clear view of how the Europeans, the best in the business, ran their race: what gears they used in the climbs, how they took turns, what kind of bicycles they rode. "The Europeans were all very tall and strong," said Hamid. "If we were motorcycles, they were 1,000cc machines, and we were 500cc."

Hamid had similar feelings about being in Japan. As the bus took the Malaysian team from Haneda Airport to the Olympic Village, he marveled at the multi-layered network of highways, the tall buildings, the billboards advertising the latest consumer technology, the trains. "My country seemed so old-fashioned to me when I came to Japan," he said.

To Asians, Japan was the shining symbol of progress and possibility in 1964.

Decades later, it is Hamid's own country, Singapore, transformed from a mosquito-infested British colony into a modern, independent business and financial center at the heart of Southeast Asia, which is now the envy of much of the world.

THE FIRST AND ONLY EVER HONG KONG OLYMPIC TEAM

They were the lowest-seeded team, and had already lost their first three matches to Malaysia, Belgium, and Canada. Their fourth match at the 1964 Tokyo Olympics was against India, a global field hockey powerhouse and a favorite to win gold.

But somehow, Hong Kong—a team of part-time players, primarily bankers who stayed fit in amateur clubs—held India scoreless in the first half of play. That would be akin to Team USA being tied 20-20 at the half in an Olympic basketball first rounder against Team Haiti, for example. In the half-time huddle, the Indian coaches and players must have been scratching their heads over why they weren't trouncing their no-name opponent.

In the second half, Hong Kong lost two of their regular defenders to injuries, and eventual gold medalist India went on to score six unanswered goals to indeed trounce the upstarts, a team that would go 0-6-1 and place fifteenth of fifteen teams in Tokyo.

India vs Hong Kong field hockey, courtesy of PHOTO KISHIMOTO

But that was OK. "The fact is," said left half Sarinder Dillon, "this was a golden opportunity to play in the Olympics. It was an honor just to be there. Maybe we'd win one or two, but just being there was great."

Dillon recalled that in late 1963 there was an outside chance Hong Kong could make the cut for the Tokyo Olympics. The Hong Kong Hockey Association told them they had better be ready just in case a team or two ahead of them dropped out.

In the subsequent months, the field hockey teams from France and Poland would indeed drop from the list, allowing the Hong Kongers to qualify. Now it was up to the players. "We were seventeen players, almost all of us bankers," said Kader Rahman, who played right half.

I worked for Bank of America, others for Hong Kong Bank, for example. And in those days, bankers played field hockey in amateur leagues. But when we realized that we had a chance at the Olympics, we worked at our offices from 9 a.m. to 5 p.m., then took a bus to King's Park and played a match every night. On Sundays, we played two matches. It was tough training for ten months, and most of the time, we still had not qualified.

Eventually, the Hong Kong Hockey Association selected thirty players from the various clubs for special training, ultimately whittling down the team to seventeen—all from different clubs. It was a very multi-cultural team, with seven Portuguese, three Indians, two Pakistanis, three Malays, an Irishman, and a Scot—all Hong Kong permanent residents. "When we walked around the Olympic Village with Hong Kong on the back of our jackets, other athletes were amazed at our team makeup," said Dillon. "We had no Chinese on the team as the few who played in Hong Kong were from the lower divisions. We all spoke English, but would sometimes talk to each other in Chinese. This further amazed the other athletes."

In addition to the training on top of their day jobs, the members of the field hockey team were tasked with raising funds themselves. The head of the Hong Kong Hockey Association, who doubled as the Olympic squad's team manager, went to many companies appealing for contributions. In the end, each team member was still required to put up a thousand Hong Kong dollars of their own money to help pay for airfare, as well as the required fee for board and lodging in the Olympic Village.

Since Dillon was a student, he was asked to pay only 130 Hong Kong dollars, which his school kindly covered. But Dillon could not escape other duties. In early September, weeks prior to the start of the Games, the Olympic torch made its way through Asia, coming to Hong Kong via Manila. As Dillon was the youngest HK Olympian, he drew the short straw and got assigned midnight guard duty of the torch, to ensure its safety before it took off for Taipei the next day.

The torch made it through the night without incident and continued its journey to Tokyo. The Hong Kong team followed shortly thereafter. Sarinder recalls his amazement at seeing his field hockey heroes from India and Pakistan in the Olympic Village, and his naiveté at thinking that the song he was repeatedly hearing was the Olympic theme, only to learn it was the American national anthem.

But awe and wonder were often blanketed by the reality of the Games. From October 11 to 18, Hong Kong lost their first six matches, scoring only two goals to the oppositions' twenty-five. Their final match was against Germany, a team made up of East Germans that would eventually place fifth in the Olympic tournament. The German team and fans in the stands were expecting a rout, a shutout, based on Hong Kong's previous matches.

Hong Kong did not comply. They scored a goal in the first half to lead the mighty Germans 1-0. In fact, they led the Germans throughout the match. With minutes to go, the players on the Hong Kong squad could taste victory, a moment all underdogs dream of—a chance to shine on the biggest stage of them all.

"We were playing a blinder, out of our usual selves," said Rahman. But then with a mere two minutes to go, Hong Kong was assessed a penalty, resulting in a short corner chance for Germany. And when the ball flew through the air toward the line of Hong Kong defenders, it somehow hit the shoulder of one of them and deflected into the goal. When the final whistle blew, it was Germany 1, Hong Kong 1.

And that was the last time a team from Hong Kong, in any sport, participated in the Games. "Our team was 100 percent amateur compared to the other countries we played," reflected Rahman. "Our results were not great, but we enjoyed our time. And today, our hockey team remains the only team from Hong Kong ever to go to the Olympics."

THE AMAZING JOURNEY OF LWRC'S ROWERS

Catch. Drive. Release. Recovery. The four phases of the rowing stroke are simple. The ability for more than two people to execute them in synch is not.

When the straight four crew from the Lake Washington Rowing Club (LWRC) arrived in Tokyo for the 1964 Summer Olympics, they were in synch and they were ready. "We believed we had a great chance to win gold," reflected Theo (Ted) Mittet (from chapter three), who sat in the bow.

As Dick Lyon, who sat in the number two seat in the shell, pointed out after winning the US Trials, the team of Ted Nash, Phil Durbrow, Lyon and Mittet were running very fast times—doing 500-meter sprints in 1 minute 27 or 28 seconds, which was better than the times Nash's gold-medal-winning team posted at the 1960 Rome Olympics.

When the crew from America lined up against Great Britain, the Netherlands, Argentina and Italy, they were raring to go. The stroke, Nash, got Team USA off to a flying start, and at the halfway mark of 1,000 meters, Nash and his team were "open water" (more than a length) up on second place Britain. The Americans had what they call "swing." Until disaster struck.

As Nash recalled in Peter Mallory's book, *The Sport of Rowing*, with the US shell comfortably ahead, the rower behind him, Durbrow, suddenly coughed up blood on and over Nash's right shoulder. Lyon said that at the 1,200-meter mark, the boat suddenly turned sideways, and he could see that Durbrow was having trouble breathing. "He was swinging in his seat and he had no power in his arms," said Lyon.

The boat came to a complete stop, but Durbrow insisted he was OK. So they got back on course and started racing past other boats until Durbrow had a second episode. Said Nash, "The guys in the bow, who could see his condition, yelled down to me, 'Phil's really hurting!'"

Mittet was in disbelief. "How could this be? What was wrong? Our feelings and concerns shifted totally to Phil in an instant—we knew that this was serious."[52]

For the crew, it was a disaster. The four from the USA still managed to cross the finish line. In fact, they completed their heat in a time of 6:56.40, over five seconds ahead of the Netherlands. Britain finished first and advanced to the finals, but because Nash's team recovered enough to finish, they were still eligible for the *repechage*, a second chance for all the crews that did not finish first in their heat.

---

52   Peter Mallory, *The Sport of Rowing*, (River & Rowing Museum, 2011), 790.

Still, Durbrow was in the hospital, to this day unsure what caused his illness. A serviceman in the US Army, Durbrow had recently done a tour in Laos, where they had given him a number of shots for various tropical diseases, and he suspects that his body suddenly rebelled against the vaccination cocktail. The team that only magically came together after trying countless variations of seventeen different people, was now forced to remake itself with an alternate, Geoff Picard, who was in Tokyo for just such a scenario. With the finals only two days away, Nash's straight four were no longer expecting to win gold, and were feeling that a medal of any color would be wishful thinking at best.

In retrospect, Durbrow understood the challenge before Picard.

> If you think about it, we rowed together for over 3,000 miles in an intense period of several months. We rowed differently from others, we had our own thing. And here comes Geoff. He was on the Harvard team we had beaten in the US Olympic Trials. He was an alternate, so he was wearing his blazer walking around the Ginza, having a gay old time...and then suddenly he's told, "You're in the boat. Get ready!"

> I sat behind Ten Nash, who was a very powerful rower. I sat behind him and my job was to even things out. Now,

suddenly, Geoff had to sit behind Ted and figure out how to fit in the best he could, in maybe two or three rowing sessions before the finals. Rowing is wonderful when there is no excess baggage. All in the boat have to act like one and think the same things and feel the same things and respond in the same way, balancing each other perfectly. They need to be aware of currents and winds and course, and the competitors—it's an incredibly complicated thing. It's like going down the highway on another car's bumper doing seventy miles per hour thinking little about it. Geoff didn't really have time to get all that.

And yet, Geoff Picard, the alternate, did.

Picard was from Harvard, training under the famed coach Harry Parker, who taught a totally different stroke technique to his rowers. According to Lyon, their own coach, Stan Pocock, taught the LWRC rowers to slow down before the catch, the moment the oar hits the water, extending their reach further than the average crew, and driving fast. The Harvard rowers were trained to be slower with the hands right after the release and faster on the catch.

In the repechage, the US coxless four (which means four rowers without a coxswain), were up against France, Japan, and Australia. France kept pace with the Americans for 1,500 meters, but the re-jigged team with Picard in the shell, pulled away in the final 150 yards to win by two boat lengths. Picard seemed to fit in well enough. But as Nash reveals in Mallory's book, "with our different west coast technique and rhythm, he told me he never totally felt in synch."

With that victory, America was heading into the finals. The reality was, the repechage was only the second time the four had rowed together—would they really be able to come together in only two days and win a medal?

In the finals on October 15, at the Toda Rowing Center, Nash, Picard, Lyon, and Mittet made a valiant effort. They fell behind quickly in the first 250 meters, in fifth behind the Netherlands, Denmark, Britain, and Germany. According to Nash, the four then began falling into synch, and started to move ahead, making up water on Denmark who had taken the lead. In fact, at the 1,500-meter mark, the US crew was actually in second, just in front of the Brits.

Theo Mittet, Dick Lyon, Geoff Picard, Ted Nash at the Toda Rowing Center, courtesy of Dick Lyon

But in the final 250 meters, the Danes held on for gold, a deserving team that had that "swing." "I could feel the water under the boat, and it sounded like music as our boat was going perfectly," said Bjorn Haslov, a member of the Danish team. "It's a strong feeling. It's a feeling that you control your body and you are a part of a team."

The Brits grabbed silver, having a bit more in the tank than the Americans. The American team, despite the calamity of Durbrow's sudden exit in the first heat, still managed to secure the bronze medal.

Nash bemoaned his tactical error in failing to get the team out aggressively at the start, which may have contributed to a loss of rhythm in the early stages. But they all knew they were fortunate to get a bronze medal. "We were very thankful to have a man of Geoff's quality as an alternate," Lyon said. "Another twenty to thirty strokes, we could have come together in time."

Durbrow remembers those mixed emotions of October 1964. "I never did see them win the bronze," he said. "I was in a pretty deep funk. I had been trying to get to the Olympics since I was sixteen, and I was in a great position to do something significant." Sadly for the rower, it wasn't to be. And to add insult to injury, the army immediately ordered him back into service in Laos.

But time heals and Durbrow has moved on, as have his teammates. One day, some fifty-two years later, Durbrow got a package in the mail. It was from Ted Nash, and inside the box was the latter's bronze medal from the 1964 Games, with a short note saying that he wanted Durbrow to have it. "Without you, our boat might not have even got to the Olympics at all."

THE BIGGEST LOSER

While so many of the 5,000 athletes who came to Tokyo in 1964 did not expect to win a medal, they did not want to be humiliated either. But in one of the most memorable sports events of the Tokyo Olympics—the men's 10,000-meter competition—a runner from Sri Lanka had placed himself in a most embarrassing situation.

Formerly a colony called British Ceylon, Sri Lanka had existed as an independent nation for only sixteen years prior to the 1964 Games, and no one from Sir Lanka was expected to win a medal. But if you weren't paying attention, you might have thought that one of their runners was battling for victory in the 10k race.

With 150 meters to go, the lead pack was jockeying for position in the home stretch, each passing a runner with the number #67. In fact everybody was passing #67, who had gotten lapped several times!

Number 67 was a slight man named Ranatunga Koralage Jayasekara Karuananda who competed in both the 5k and 10k races in Tokyo. After getting lapped in the first 1,000 meters of the 10k race, he continued to fall off the pace. When the eventual winner flared wide and put on a burst of speed to win dramatically in the final meters, Karuananda had a perfect view, only meters behind. But while the winner ended his race in elation, Karuananda crossed the finish line knowing he was last...with four more long laps to go. He could have stopped. If he did, he would have joined the nine others who did not finish, and no one would have noticed.

Instead, the officer in the Sri Lanka Army, known to friends as Karu, plodded on.

The spectators at first were bewildered. Wasn't the race over? Why was this guy still running...and running...and running? And yet, as Karuananda ran, the crowd noise went from ambivalence to encouragement. With three laps to go, the crowd began cheering the lone competitor as he made his way around the stadium track.

The winner of the race wanted so much to take a victory lap around the stadium but was thwarted by a Japanese official who told him to stay put. After all, the race was still on. Instead of the gold medalist, here was the last place finisher bathing in the growing cheers of 70,000, who likely only minutes before learned that #67 was Karuananda of Sri Lanka.

And when Karuananda rounded the last turn, he sprinted down the straightaway, crossing the finish line to a standing ovation and a thunderous cheer, as if he had just snatched his island's first medal.

It is said that Karuananda told reporters at the Olympic Village that he was only doing what was expected of an Olympian. "The Olympic spirit is not to win, but to take part. So I came here. I took part in the 10,000 meters and completed my rounds."

Karu became an overnight star in Japan, his desire to complete the race a symbol of the core value of perseverance so central to Japan's successful rise from the rubble. Karu represented every hardworking man and woman in Japan, and they loved him for that.

HIGH JUMPER ED CARUTHERS AND HIS JOURNEY FROM TOKYO TO MEXICO CITY

Still a freshman at Santa Ana College, high jumper Ed Caruthers was headed to the Tokyo Olympics in 1964. Caruthers had always been a football player, and as a pretty good wide receiver/defensive back, he hoped one day to get drafted by an NFL team. Out of football season, Caruthers dabbled in track and field. Strangely, with little effort, Caruthers would win most high jump competitions. In 1964, he said he "went to the AAU championships, and lo and behold, I jumped seven-feet-one-inch, and beat John Thomas, the best American high jumper at the time, which then qualified me for the Olympic trials."

Even more strangely, Caruthers wasn't even aware that the Olympics were being held that year. He was simply more interested in preparing for the football season that fall. But when he won the finals in the high jump at the Olympic trials in September, he realized that if he were going to the Olympics, he wasn't going to play football for Santa Ana in the coming months, and so did not register for school. As he said, his track coach was "happy as a lark," while his football coach had a hole in his team.

So Caruthers the football player, who ended up being an accidental Olympian, took off for Japan in early October, about a week in advance of the opening ceremonies. Caruthers was in good shape when he arrived, but with so much time before his competition, he needed to train. Unfortunately, American high jumpers did not have dedicated coaches. And for whatever reason, the veterans on the team did not reach out to the kid from Oklahoma City.

The high jump competition was in the last two or three days, so I was in Tokyo three weeks without competition. I didn't have any coaching, and I didn't go up to any coach and ask them either. I'm jumping by myself, so I didn't have that extra thing to push me higher. If John Rambo or John Thomas were out there training with me, I might have had the adrenaline going, wanting to show them. But (even though we were teammates) I was a competitor to them, so we didn't.

Caruthers was not born of wealth and was barely eating a bowl of cereal a day when he was a student in junior college. But when he came to Tokyo, and was privy to the bounty of the Olympic Village, he ended up eating eggs, waffles, bacon, cookies, ice cream, and lots of it. "I weighed 190 pounds when I arrived. After two weeks, I weighed 198 pounds. I thought maybe when you go to the other side of the world you gain weight, but no." He just ate too much.

So prior to the high jump competition, Caruthers stopped eating. For three days, all he consumed was cornflakes, milk, and salad. Predictably, he was not feeling as strong as he wanted to at the start of the competition, nor as right or ready. As a consequence, Caruthers did not perform the way he had expected.

> I was getting up really good but I couldn't tell what I was doing wrong. People in the stands who saw me jump said, "We can't believe you missed that...all you had to do is step one foot back." I was about three to four inches over the bar. My plant wasn't in the right place but I couldn't tell. I'm nineteen years old. The first jump was easy. But you have to make adjustments in your second or third jumps. At seven feet everything has to be really refined and precise—there's less room for error. I needed to make adjustments. After my second attempt I really needed someone to tell me, but all I'm doing is I'm trying to run faster because I think I need more effort. I ended up jumping only 6-10 and a quarter.

Caruthers finished in eighth place. He sat on the bench and watched the others compete to the finish. Valeriy Brumel of the Soviet Union and John Thomas both jumped 2.16 meters (about seven feet one inch) but could not go beyond that. Brumel took gold on fewer misses, Thomas silver, and Rambo bronze. Caruthers thought, "Damn, there are two guys on the medal stand I've beaten this year. There's no reason I shouldn't be on that stand."

He thought about the opening ceremonies, being together with thousands of athletes, all the flags of the world flapping around him, and "I'm right there in the middle of it. I am with the best athletes in the world." He realized at his darkest moment that finishing eighth was not good enough, that his attitude and focus were inadequate, and that he wanted, needed to redeem himself in Mexico City four years later.

When Caruthers returned home to California, he was determined to focus more on track than on football. He was offered scholarships to play at USC or UCLA, but he picked the University of Arizona because it was 500 miles away from home, and from all the distractions of his friends and neighborhood. And he also wanted to make sure that he got his degree and sought help from the university to ensure that he did well with his grades and graduated.

> That's what Tokyo did for me. Prior to that I only cared about two weeks from now. After Tokyo, my attitude was the difference between night and day. Training. Confidence. Everything. I knew what I was in school for. I had a schedule. I built up my strength. I refined my technique. I worked it so that I knew exactly what I should be doing to jump my best height.

In 1967, there was no better high jumper in the world

than Ed Caruthers. He was primed for gold in Mexico City. He was determined. Nothing was to get in the way of his goal—to erase the memory of his poor performance in Tokyo. Nothing.

Nothing...except a guy named Dick Fosbury, who revolutionized the high jumping sport with his amazingly awkward head-first, face up technique. Caruthers won silver behind the Fosbury Flop in Mexico City. But it was a silver born of hard lessons learned in Tokyo.

CHAPTER 6

SACRIFICING FOR THE GREATER GOOD

SUCCESS COMES WITH A PRICE

SWEDEN TO THE RESCUE

In pursuit of a greater good, there is often sacrifice, both big and small. In a Japanese culture that prioritizes the group over the individual, keeping personal preferences and needs submerged in order to cater to the perceived interests of the neighborhood, classmates, team members, or colleagues at work are calculations of emotional and social intelligence that Japanese make every day.

To the Japanese, the sacrifices the individual must make

to the group are most often seen as praiseworthy, symbolic of a powerful value in Japanese society.

At the 1964 Olympics, there were two sailors who came in eighteenth overall in a sailing category called the Flying Dutchman (FD) competition. But they came in first in the hearts of the Japanese.

On October 14, Stig Lennart Käll and his younger brother, Lars Gunnar Käll, in their boat Hayama, were sailing in the third race of seven in the FD-class competition when they saw a capsized boat ahead of them, and the two crew members floating in the middle of Sagami Bay.

Making a quick decision, the Käll brothers steered their way toward Australian sailor Ian Charles Winter, and plucked him out of the water. They then proceeded to the capsized Australian boat, Diablo, to rescue the second member of that crew, John Gregory Dawe, and pulled him into their boat as well. In addition to the Australians, six other boats failed to complete the race, which likely meant rough conditions. And yet, the Swedes, with two extra passengers, still managed to finish the heat.

The exploits of the Swedish crew were publicized nationally in the Japanese press. Fans from all over the country sent a barrage of letters and gifts of appreciation to the two Swedish sailors who were singled out for their sacrifice to the greater good.

It was also well publicized that the captain of the Japanese women's volleyball team was making a sacrifice for the good of her volleyball team, as well as for the country. At the age of thirty-one, the team captain, Masae Kasai, was older by about six or seven years than most of her teammates. She had intended to retire from volleyball and get married after leading her team to Japan's first World Championship in a victory over the Soviet Union in 1962. In fact, some felt that Kasai's duty to Japanese society, as a woman, was to get married and have children, not to play volleyball. Kasai herself made it clear she wanted to move on and start a family.

But in the end, the call for gold and glory for Japan at the 1964 Tokyo Olympics was so strong that she decided to delay retirement, and thus surrender herself to two more years of long, punishing hours in the gym. Her sacrifice was eventually rewarded, however, as she did make it to the altar in a highly publicized wedding after the Games ended.

Another story was that of Takashi Ono, the legendary veteran gymnast from Akita, Japan, who had already garnered twelve medals (including four golds) from the 1952, 1956, and 1960 Olympiads. At thirty-three, Ono was the oldest member of the 1964 team.

Ono's strongest discipline was the horizontal bar. It was vital he did his best to give his team a chance for gold. But Ono was in considerable pain due to a right shoulder injured in his preparations for the Olympics. To ease the discomfort, he was injected with an anesthetic, which resulted in the loss of feeling in his entire arm.

According to Rio Otomo, who wrote about the gymnast in her article, *Narratives of the Body and the 1964 Tokyo Olympics*, Ono's injury was a major narrative of the Olympics, one also taken up by famed writer Yukio Mishima:

> The horizontal bar had been cruelly attacking his shoulder for some time. His shoulder then became the enemy of the perfection that Ono was aiming to achieve. It was assaulting him from within, as if it had been a spy who sold his soul to the enemy camp.[53]

Less known to the public were the apprehensions of Ono's wife and teammate on the women's gymnastics team. As Otomo wrote, Kiyoko Ono was concerned that attempting difficult maneuvers in the air with a damaged arm could result in a terrible fall, and so she whispered to her husband as he approached the bar, "Please do not die; we have children."

---

53   Rio Otomo, "Narratives, the Body and the 1964 Tokyo Olympics," *Asian Studies Review*, 31 (June 2007): 123.

Takashi and Kiyoko Ono in dining hall, courtesy of PHOTO KISHIMOTO

Not only did Ono survive, the grit he showed that day helped lead his team to the gold medal.

But of all the stories of pain and sacrifice at the 1964 Summer Games, perhaps the most poignant was the story of marathoner Kokichi Tsuburaya.

THE MARATHON SPRINT THAT BROKE THE HEARTS OF THE JAPANESE

Abebe Bikila entered the National Stadium like he owned it. The lithe Ethiopian, a member of the Imperial Bodyguard of his nation, was about to meet expectations at the 1964 Tokyo Olympics—to become the first person to win marathons in two consecutive Olympiads.

The first time Bikila won, he was an unknown, and made headlines by running barefoot on the roads of Rome in 1960 to take gold. When he crossed the finish line in Tokyo, amazingly over four minutes ahead of the second-place finisher, the audience erupted in applause, and marveled at how fresh Bikila was—so fresh in fact that he did calisthenics and jogged in place as if he were readying for the start of a second marathon.

Abebe Bikila, courtesy of PHOTO KISHIMOTO

The fact that Bikila was so far and away in a class by himself meant that the real competition in the marathon was for second. And in the race for second, Japan was ready to explode in celebration.

At the 10k mark of the 42k race, Ron Clarke of Australia was setting a pretty fast pace at 30:14, with Jim Hogan of

Ireland and Bikila following. Around the 20k mark, Bikila took the lead and never looked back. The race for second was on, with Clarke and Hogan about five seconds behind Bikila, and a second pack including the Japanese runner, Kokichi Tsuburaya, and Jozsef Suto of Hungary.

With about seven kilometers to go, Bikila, Hogan, Tsuburaya, and Suto were in front of the pack, with a British runner named Basil Heatley rising to fifth. Heatley remembers the humidity, sweat dripping from his body even before the race began. Hogan, dehydrated and exhausted, dropped out of the race despite being in second due to the conditions. Heatley decided that he would not try to race to the front, instead staying comfortably back.

Keeping to a moderate pace because of the heat, and bothered by a cramp near his left ribcage, Heatley was two-and-a-half minutes off the lead pack, when his teammate Brian Kilby, came alongside, lifting Heatley's spirit. "I had great respect for Brian Kilby's pace judgment and expected him to be a medalist. Therefore, to be running alongside Brian was a positive. At that point, I knew I would finish the race, but had little idea of where we were placed, although I knew I was moving up the field."

Heatley was advancing and started to envision a bronze-medal finish behind the Japanese runner. "I didn't expect to catch him," he said, "but he was a target."

Shortly after Bikila had finished his cooling-down exercises, Tsuburaya entered the stadium and the crowd went wild. At their home Olympics, Japan had medaled in wrestling, judo, boxing, weightlifting, gymnastics, and swimming, among others, but not in track and field. Tsuburaya was about to change that with perhaps the most significant silver medal at the Games in front of the biggest crowd he had ever experienced.

And yet, soon after Tsuburaya entered the stadium, so, too, did Heatley, only seconds behind. The Brit knew this was his chance. "Fifteen years of racing told me that, at that moment, an injection of pace was necessary, and possible, to overtake the runner in front of me," he said. Just before the final curve of the stadium's cinder track, Heatley turned on the jets and sprinted by his rival. For a battle that took over two hours and sixteen minutes, Tsuburaya lost his chance for silver by four seconds.

Kokichi Tsuburaya and Basil Heatley, courtesy of PHOTO KISHIMOTO

Writer Robert Whiting was watching the event on television, confident that Tsuburaya would make Japan proud with a silver medal only to see that expectation burst before the eyes of an entire nation, as he explained in The Japan Times:[54]

> The cheering for Tsuburaya was building to a crescendo when suddenly Great Britain's Basil Heatley came into view and proceeded to put on one of Olympic track and field's great all-time spurts. He steadily closed the gap in the last 100 meters, passing Tsuburaya shortly before the wire, turning the wild cheering in the coffee shop, and in the stadium, and no doubt in the rest of Japan, into one huge collective groan.

---

54   Robert Whiting, "Schollander, Hayes Were Spectacular at Tokyo Games," *The Japan Times*, October 17, 2014.

Bob Schul, who three days earlier became the first American to win gold in the 5,000-meter race, watched the end of the marathon with his wife, Sharon.

> Abebe entered the stadium to great applause. He finished and went into the infield and started doing exercises. Finally, the second guy, Tsuburaya came, and the crowd roared. But so did Heatley of England. Sharon asked if Tsuburaya could hold on to second place. I said I didn't think so. Heatley caught him about 150 meters before the finish. And the crowd became very quiet. The Japanese guy was going to get third. And when he did finish, the stadium did erupt.

Tsuburaya's very public loss of the silver medal must have been painful, not only for the runner himself, but for the nation as a whole. Still, Tsuburaya's run supplied one of the Games' highlights for Japan. His bronze was Japan's only medal in track and field, an achievement beyond the nation's initial expectations. Writer Hitomi Yamaguchi wrote of this pain and pride in a 1964 article:

> Tsuburaya tried so very hard. And his efforts resulted in the raising of the Japanese flag in the National Stadium. My chest hurt. I applauded so much I didn't take any notes. Since the start of the Olympic Games, our national flag had not risen once in the National Stadium. At this last event, we were about to have a record of no medals in track and

field. Kon Ishikawa's film cameras were rolling, and newspaper reporters were watching. People were waiting and hoping. So when Tsubaraya crossed the finish line, we felt so fortunate! When I saw the Japanese flag raised freely into the air, it felt fantastic. Tsuburaya, thank you.[55]

When Kokichi Tsuburaya was a boy in elementary school, he participated in an event common throughout Japan—a sports day, when children compete against each other in a variety of activities, like foot races. After one such race, Koshichi Tsuburaya, the young runner's father, chewed him out for looking behind him during the race. "Why are you looking back? Looking back is a bad thing. If you believe in yourself, you don't need to do that."

Many years later, with the crowd of over 70,000 on its feet and cheering, at the showcase event of the Olympics, people were yelling, "Tsuburaya, a runner is behind you! Look back! Look back! He's close!"[56] At that moment, was Tsuburaya recalling that childhood scolding from his father? Was he letting down his father? His family? His nation?

---

55 Hitomi Yamaguchi, "Tsuburaya, Arigatou," Houchi Shimbun, October 22, 1964, in *Tokyo Olympic—Bungakusha ni Yoru Tokyo Gorin Zenkiroku* (Kodansha; 2015), 162.

56 Ichiro Aoyama, "Kokou no Rannaa—Kokichi Tsuburaya Monogatari (The Lone Runner—The Kokichi Tsuburaya Story)" *Baseball Magazine* (2008), 26.

NEVER GIVE UP!

Do your best. Persevere. Never give up.

Ganbare! Akirameru na!

These are values that resonate with the Japanese. You see it in the office worker who stays late to get things done, night after night. You see it in the high school baseball player who dives left and right after dozens if not hundreds of ground balls in the rain. You see it in the artist who tirelessly works the pottery wheel until she gets the exact curvature in the clay she sees in her head.

Kokichi Tsuburaya exemplified those values. And when he drove toward the finish line of the grueling 42-kilometer marathon, spent but on the verge of grabbing silver, urged on by the cheers of a nation, he was giving it his all.

Watching the marathon, courtesy of PHOTO KISHIMOTO

When Heatley accelerated past the depleted Tsuburaya like a biker passing a pedestrian, the growing balloon of hope of an entire nation seemed to deflate in those seconds it took Heatley to get to the finish line.

Tsuburaya was a proud athlete. Whatever he may have been feeling on the inside, he took the loss of the silver medal stoically, determined to do better. As he said in interviews after the marathon, "I will practice hard toward Mexico City."

Needless to say, Tsuburaya was a product of his national culture. But more relevantly, he was his father's son, as explained in Ichiro Aoyama's book, *The Other Side of Glory and Loneliness-The Kokichi Tsuburaya Story.*[57]

The seven children in the Tsuburaya household had to work hard, cleaning the house, preparing the bath, cooking, planting the rice, and raising the livestock when they hit the age of ten. These were not easy tasks, and the head of the household, Koshichi Tsuburaya, believed that his children needed to be disciplined to ensure they did their chores, and that doing these things properly would allow them to stand up on their own two feet when they grew up.

As a child, Kokichi liked to run, and when his dog ran here

---

57   Ichiro Aoyama, "Eikō to Kodoku no Kanata e Tsuburaya Kōkichi Monogatari (The Other Side of Glory and Loneliness—The Kokichi Tsuburaya Story)" *Baseball Magazine* (1992), 22.

and there, little Kokichi strove to keep up with it. But one day when he was five, Kokichi felt a sharp pain in his legs and his back. The father then noticed that the boy's left leg was shorter than his right. Knowing how little their Kokichi would complain about anything, the parents took him to the hospital, where they learned that their boy also had tuberculosis arthritis, which causes pain in the weight-bearing joints of the hips, knees, and ankles. So from an early age, Kokichi felt pain whenever he ran.

And yet, he looked up to his older brother, who ran competitively. Kokichi often joined him, and the elder sibling was surprised to see his kid brother keeping up, despite being seven years younger. The two would often go for runs in the evenings. But their father didn't approve of running for the sake of running. "You can't live off of running," he would say as a warning to his sons, and repeat the refrain every time they came in late from an evening run. In order to avoid their father's glare, the boys took to sneaking out for a run while Koshichi was in the bath.

Finally one night, Koshichi the father confronted Kokichi the son and asked him, "If you run, will you stick to it?" The boy said yes, to which the father said, in the approving way of gruff dads, "Once you decide to do this, don't quit halfway through."

Kokichi never quit. In fact, he took his commitment to

running very seriously. In high school, he trained very hard for a national 5,000-meter competition, with the support of a high school teacher who also ran middle distance. They encouraged each other to compete in the big race, but the teacher, Hisashi Saito, was eliminated in the preliminary stages, and Kokichi decided to run and win for his teacher.

He did not win, which was to be expected for a newcomer to the national stage. And yet, Kokichi felt bad for letting his teacher down, and apologized before him with tears running down his cheeks. And so he decided to show accountability in a traditional and public way—he shaved his head.

When Kokichi graduated from high school, he did something that made his father proud—he joined the Ground Self-Defense Force and became a soldier as his father had been. Japan has a long tradition of long-distance relay races, and Kokichi was slated to join the team representing the Self-Defense Force in a national long-distance race. At the time of the race, however, he was in the hospital with a high fever. On top of that, he kept secret the fact that a slipped disk in his back was also causing him tremendous pain. Despite all that, Kokichi Tsuburaya insisted on running the longest leg of the race.

It was this commitment, this perseverance that endeared

Tsuburaya to the public—and that won over his father, who had once believed that nothing would come of his son's running. His father would often send him letters filled with encouragement, but at the same time expressing concern for his son's well-being. And when Kokichi returned home from his bronze-medal finish at the Olympics, he discovered that his parents kept all sorts of news clippings, medals, and trophies of his accomplishments. He was surprised to learn that his parents could not sleep on the eve of the Olympics, and worried deeply about his health.

THE SUICIDE

Tsuburaya was a man of commitment, and he promised he would work hard to ensure he was ready to compete and do better at the 1968 Olympics in Mexico City. Not only did he feel the need to make up for the "loss" of silver, so too did his seniors at Japan's Ground Self-Defense Force.

Tsuburaya did indeed train hard. And yet, somehow, he also found time for courtship. He met a girl named Eiko before the Tokyo Olympics, and he wanted to marry her after the Tokyo Games. His coach at the Self-Defense Force athletics school, Hiro Hatano, was supportive of the proposed marriage. Tsuburaya's parents, too, approved of their son's plans.

But in 1966, coach Hatano's reporting officer expressed his dissatisfaction with the union, saying that the next Olympics was more important than getting married. He thought it was so important that Tsuburaya focus 100 percent on his training that he brought Hatano, Tsuburaya's father, Eiko and Eiko's mother together to inform them that the marriage to Tsuburaya would have to wait until after the Games. Tsuburaya was not present in that meeting.

Eiko was devoted to Tsuburaya and wanted to wait until they could get married. But Eiko's mother was no longer supportive.[58]

In the end, the proposed marriage was broken off. Tsuburaya's coach and manager, Hatano, was left with the unfortunate task of informing Tsuburaya. Hatano protested these decisions to his own boss to the point where he ended up being demoted and removed as Tsuburaya's coach. The runner was thus left to train on his own, likely feeling quite alone. Very quickly, injuries began to plague him—first the return of the intense pain of the slipped disc, and then an injury to an Achilles tendon, which required surgery in 1967.

At the end of 1967, Tsuburaya returned to his hometown of Sukagawa, Fukushima, for the long holiday break that

58   Ichiro Aoyama, "Eikō to Kodoku no Kanata e Tsuburaya Kōkichi Monogatari," 266.

bridges the old year with the new. Tsuburaya's father was pained with news that he wasn't sure he should share with his son. But he decided it would be best to tell him before he found out on his own—that his former fiancé, Eiko, had gotten married. Kokichi replied, "Oh, Eiko-san is married. That's good for her." He pretended that he was OK with the news, but his father could tell that his son was shocked and saddened.[59]

Tsuburaya returned to his Self-Defense Force base after his time with family during the New Year's break. And on January 8, 1968, he slit his wrists and died in his dorm room.

A SUICIDE NOTE QUINTESSENTIALLY JAPANESE

My dear Father, my dear Mother, I enjoyed the delicious three-day tororo soup, the dried persimmons, and the rice cakes.

My dear Brother Toshio, and my dear Sister, I enjoyed the delicious sushi.

My dear Brother Katsumi, and my dear Sister, I enjoyed the delicious wine and apples.

My dear Brother Iwao, and my dear Sister, I enjoyed the delicious shiso herbal rice, and the nanban zuke pickles.

---

59   Ichiro Aoyama, "Eikō to Kodoku no Kanata e Tsuburaya Kōkichi Monogatari," 309.

My dear Brother Kikuzo, and my dear Sister, I enjoyed the delicious grape juice and Yomeishu wine. I enjoyed them. And thank you, my dear Sister, for the laundry you always did for me.

My dear Brother Kozo and my dear Sister, I thank you for the rides you gave me in your car, to and fro. I enjoyed the delicious mongo-cuttlefish.

My dear Brother Masao, and my dear Sister, I am very sorry for all the worries I caused you.

Sachio-kun, Hideo-kun, Mikio-kun, Toshiko-chan, Hideko-chan, Ryosuke-kun, Takahisa-kun, Miyoko-chan, Yukie-chan, Mitsue-chan, Akira-kun, Yoshiyuki-kun, Keiko-chan, Koei-kun, Yu-chan, Kii-chan, Shoji-kun: May you grow up to be fine people.

My dear Father and my dear Mother, your Kokichi is too tired to run anymore. Please forgive him. He is sorry to have worried you all the time.

My dear Father and Mother, Kokichi would have liked to have lived by your side.

These were the handwritten words of Tsubaraya, one of two notes he left as explanation for why he took his life.

Suicide rates, while decreasing in recent years, have been

traditionally high in Japan compared to other countries. Anecdotal evidence suggests there may be a certain romanticism connected with suicide in Japan. So when some of Japan's most celebrated writers, Yukio Mishima and Nobel Laureate Yasunari Kawabata, among others, read the suicide note of Kokichi Tsuburaya, they swooned at the simple yet striking words of this athlete. Mishima viewed Tsuburaya's notes as "beautiful, honest, and sad." And as Makoto Ueda explained in his book, *Modern Japanese Writers and the Nature of Literature*, Kawabata was even jealous of the quality of Tsuburaya's poetry.

> Kawabata was deeply moved upon reading this suicide note. After citing it in its entirety, he offered to explain why: "in the simple, plain style and in the context of the emotion-ridden note, the stereotyped phase 'I enjoyed' is breathing with truly pure life. It creates a rhythm pervading the entire suicide note. It is beautiful, sincere, and sad." Kawabata then observed that this suicide note was not inferior to similar notes written by reputable writers, despite the fact that Tsuburaya was an athlete who boasted no special talent in composition. Kawabata even felt ashamed of his own writings, he said, when he compared them with this note.

Mishima, in 1970, and Kawabata, in 1972, would also take their own lives.

Another giant of Japanese literature and Nobel Laureate, Kenzaburo Oe, was also impressed by Tsuburaya's last words. At a series of talks Oe gave at the University of California, Berkeley, in April 1999, he explained at length how Tsuburaya's suicide note was a striking cultural marker of the 1960s, a reflection of Japan in a state of transition during a period of intense social, economic, and political change—more specifically, from large to nuclear families, from fresh to frozen foods, from famine to feast, from obedience to rebellion.[60]

> We know from this note that Kokichi Tsuburaya was from a big family. The many names he mentions probably do not evoke any particular feeling in a non-Japanese, but to a person like myself—especially to one who belongs to an older generation of Japanese—these names reveal the naming ideology of a family in which authority centers around the paternal head of household. This family-ism extends to the relatives. There is probably no large family in Japan today where children are named so thoroughly in line with traditional ethical sentiments. Tsuburaya's suicide note immediately shows the changes in the "feelings" of the families of Japanese these past thirty years.

Professor Shunya Yoshimi of The University of Tokyo conducted an online course called, Visualizing Postwar Tokyo, in which he highlighted the stress that people

---

60   Kenzaburo Oe, "On Politics and Literature: Two Lectures by Kenzaburo Oe," *Occasional Papers of the Doreen B. Townsend Center*, no. 18 (1999): 39.

in Japan, particularly in Tokyo, were under due to the rapid socio-economic change taking place. He shared the opening minutes of a 1963 NHK documentary called "Tokyo," by director Naoya Yoshida, which shows the crowds, the noise, the traffic, and the construction through the eyes of a woman whose father was killed in the Tokyo fire bombings and whose mother ran away from home.

> Tokyo, unplanned and full of construction sites, is no place for a human being to live. Only a robot with no sense could live in this rough, coarse, harsh, and dusty city that doesn't have any blue skies. Many people complain like this. But I disagree. I think this city is just desperately hanging along, just like me.

Oe continued to explain in his talk that Japan in the mid-to-late 1960s was experiencing fractures in the veneer of optimism and need for harmony and perseverance that had propelled the country into its great Olympic year, as traditional relationships and ways of thinking began to break down. Tsuburaya, according to Oe, could no longer bear the rifts in society.

> Domestically, 1968 saw the rage of student rebellions, most noted among which were the struggles at Tokyo University and Nihon University. Outside of Japan, there was the May Revolution in Paris, and the invasion of Soviet troops into

Prague. In retrospect, we clearly see that the world was full of premonitions of great change.

Against this backdrop, a long-distance runner of the Self-Defense Forces—itself a typical phenomenon of the state of postwar Japan's twisted polysemous society—turned his back on the currents of such a society, alone prepared to die, and wrote this suicide note. In the note, the young man refers to specific foods and drinks, he encourages his nephews and nieces to grow up to be fine people; he is overwhelmed by the thought of his parents' loving concern for him and writes that he knows their hearts must never have rested in their worry and care for him. He apologizes to them because, having kept running even after the Olympics with the aim of shouldering national prestige, he became totally exhausted and could no longer run. He closed his note with the words: "My dear Father and Mother, Kokichi would have liked to live by your side."[61]

Tsuburaya was a man of his era, celebrated in 1964 for his accomplishments as an athlete. Today he is also remembered for his eloquence, a poet who is said to have captured the essence and the angst of those times.

---

61 Kenzaburo Oe, "On Politics and Literature: Two Lectures by Kenzaburo Oe," *Occasional Papers of the Doreen B. Townsend Center*, no. 18 (1999): 40.

CHAPTER 7

KONJO

YOU MUST NOT GIVE UP

If you think your opponent is stronger than you and get the jitters, or if you are in a difficult position and feel that you must give up, then it will be impossible for you to win. You must not give up the bout until the last second, no matter how strong your opponent may be. You must have a fighting spirit which will urge you on to attack and attack again to the very end.

—ISAO INOKUMA, GOLD MEDALIST IN THE JUDO
HEAVYWEIGHT DIVISION, 1964 TOKYO OLYMPICS[62]

For many American adults, the men's ice hockey semi-finals between the USA and the USSR at the Lake Placid Olympics in 1980, and particularly the call of Al Michaels

---

62   Isao Inokuma, "Fighting Spirit," *JudoInfo.com*.

as the seconds ticked down in the US upset victory—"Do you believe in miracles? YES!"—are etched indelibly in memory.

For many Japanese adults in 1964, memories of a twenty-two-year-old swimmer named Hideko Maehata were still fresh. Maehata had brought back a silver medal in the 200-meter breaststroke at the 1932 Los Angeles Olympics, losing gold by a tenth of a second. She returned to Japan a heroine, and the press debated whether she should marry, as was customary for a Japanese woman at the time, or go for gold at the 1936 Berlin Olympics.

The mayor of Tokyo, Hidejiro Nagata, was hoping to show the world that Japan was on equal terms with the West by securing the 1940 Olympics for Japan, so he personally encouraged Maehata to go to Berlin and win. "If only you had won that gold medal," he told her. "It must be so frustrating. Don't forget that bitter taste of defeat. Let it drive you to do better four years from now in Berlin."[63]

Maehata understood that she had to try to win gold for Japan, and committed to a grueling training regimen. But she would be facing a strong competitor in a German swimmer named Martha Genenger. Could she beat the German in her own country? Could she bear the weight of an entire nation that was counting on her to show the

63   NHK, "World Begin Japanology Hideko Maehata" (video).

world that Japan was a nation to be respected, not only in Asia but in the West as well?

In 1936, as explained in Robin Kietlinski's book, *Japanese Women and Sport*, radio was a rising medium, providing news and entertainment directly to Japanese homes throughout the country. NHK, the government broadcaster, decided to transmit the call of the 200-meter finals live from Berlin. Sansei Kasai was the announcer on the scene, and he provided a call that thrilled listeners all over Japan, particularly the oft-repeated phrase: "*Maehata ganbare!*" or "Go (for it) Maehata!"

> Go for it Maehata! (Repeated four times) Twenty-five meters left to go! Maehata's lead is small, it's very small! Maehata! Go for it Maehata! (Repeated eleven times) Maehata is in the lead! (Repeated six times) Five meters left to go! Four meters left! Three meters! Two meters! Maehata is ahead! Maehata has won! (Repeated eighteen times) Maehata is the champion! Thank you Maehata, the Japanese flag will fly today! Thank you! For the first time in the history of women's swimming the Japanese flag will fly![64]

The first Japanese woman to win gold at the Olympics instantly became the most famous person in Japan. Maehata represented "possibility," one who, with a bit of

---

64 Robin Kietlinski, *Japanese Women and Sport: Beyond Baseball and Sumo*, (London: Bloomsbury Academic, 2011), 72-73.

moxie and a lot of hard work, could do anything. Maehata had *"konjo,"* a particularly resonant value in Japan—the will and the guts to persevere. More than two decades after her victory, she remained a perfect sports symbol for the Japanese, who were striving in their Everyday Olympics as office workers, bus drivers, factory line workers, waitresses, and construction workers to bring Japan back from the dead. Reminded by Kasai's ringing voice in the lead up to the Tokyo Olympics, the Japanese were primed to see their underdog athletes give it their all, and on occasion, stand on the top podium, and see their flag fly.

In 1964, other Japanese athletes would assume Maehata's mantle, but *"konjo"* was certainly not a value unique to Japan. Billy Mills, Dawn Fraser, and Dick Roth also showed the world that, where there's a will, there's a way.

AIMLESS AND ANGRY

It was a very hot day, and I was running in the back of the pack. As I came by coach Easton he said, "Billy, get up where you belong; get up in front." Another lap went by, and I heard him say, or I thought I heard him say, "Get up where you belong or get off the track." And I thought: You know, there's a third way to do this, and it's my way. I'm a senior in college. I can do it my way, which is to run in the back and come up slowly.

When Easton said that again, I walked off the track. He sent for me and said, "Why did you quit?" I answered, "Coach, I didn't quit. You said to get up in front or get off the track. I got off the track."

"You quit," he said. All the pressures I was feeling I took out on this man who was really trying to help me. By walking off the track I may have appeared to be protesting against my coach, but in reality I was protesting against society. I don't think he ever understood that.[65]

Billy Mills, who would later take the world by surprise at the 1964 Tokyo Olympics, was an angry young man, as you can tell from his own words, published in the book, *Tales of Gold*. A Native American of the Lakota tribe, he developed into such a strong distance runner that he earned a scholarship to Kansas University, where Mills struggled with life outside the reservation.

Bill Easton was the coach of the track team at Kansas. During his tenure there, 1947 to 1965, his track teams won conference championships eight years in a row from 1952 to 1959. By the time Billy Mills met the KU coach, Easton had the supreme confidence that comes from consistently winning. And yet, Mills and Easton were like oil and water. Mills felt that Easton was a symbol of all the

65   Lewis H. Carlson and John H. Fogarty, Tales of Gold: An Oral History of the Summer Olympic Games Told by America's Gold Medal Winners (Contemporary Books Inc., 1987), 348.

barriers society put in his way, and after the altercation described above, Mills quit the track team.

> I had a love-hate relationship with Easton. I wanted to please him, but I wanted to do things my way, the way I knew was best for me. And the hostility that grew out of all the blatant and subtle rejections that society was throwing at me I took out on him, and he really had no idea I was doing that. I was trying to find answers to questions I couldn't even express, and my coach was not a sociologist or a psychologist. He couldn't determine where I was coming from. So during my years at Kansas my track career languished.[66]

In the 1983 film, *Running Brave*, actor Robbie Benson portrays Billy Mills as an intense and tightly wound young man, who hides his emotions behind ambiguous smiles and blank expressions, only to let them out in raw displays of frustration and anger, usually in private.

When, in the film, Easton comes out to Mills's high school to see him run, and learns that Mills is Native American, Easton tells the high school coach, within earshot of Mills, "You know as well as I do what happens to these Indian boys. They are gifted runners, but they can't take orders. They have no discipline. They're quitters! Sooner or later,

---

66 Lewis H. Carlson and John H. Fogarty, *Tales of Gold*, 348.

they all end up back at the reservation pumping gas or dead drunk, or on skid row. You know that."

When Mills's Kansas University track team is invited to go to a fraternity party, he goes along with the joy of a first-time experience, only to be told that Indians aren't allowed in the fraternity. When he begins dating a Caucasian co-ed at Kansas, he grows frustrated that the parents of his girlfriend, later his wife, Pat, did not openly accept him initially.

> In retrospect, I can understand now that some of that might have been not because I was an Indian, but because here I was, an orphan, raised in poverty, and the prospect that their daughter might have some security with me was very slim. But at the time, I understood that they didn't want their daughter to have anything to do with an Indian, even a part Indian.[67]

Mills was eight when his mother died—bewildered, scared, and angry. His father told little Billy that he had to look beyond his fear and his anger, because those emotions could destroy him. "You have broken wings," his father said. "You need a dream to fix broken wings. Find your dreams son. It is the pursuit of your dreams that will heal you. If you do this you may have the wings of an eagle."

---

67   Lewis H. Carlson and John H. Fogarty, *Tales of Gold*, 347.

Shortly after that, his father told him of a book about the Olympics, saying that, "Olympians are chosen by the Gods." Inspired by that thought, Mills believed that if he became an Olympian, if he were chosen by the Gods, "Maybe I'd be able to see my mom again."

Mills is clearly a spiritual person. He knows his parents, both of whom passed away when he was young, are looking over him. He believes in his darkest times that they are there to guide him. When he was attending the University of Kansas, his first attempt to live outside the reservation, he struggled to fit in. Mills said that at one point in his time at KU he was feeling desperate, in fact, feeling as if the best solution was to take his own life.

"I was a junior in college, and on the verge of suicide," he said. "I was in my room, standing on a chair and was about to jump out my window. But I started hearing energy. Underneath my skin, I felt energy that sounded like a word: 'Don't.' It sounded like my dad's voice."

Mills was shaken out of his desperation by this surprise message from his father. He stepped down from the chair and decided that suicide was not the answer. He recalled what his father told him when his mother died—that the pursuit of a dream heals broken souls. And that's when Mills wrote down his dream on a piece of paper:

Gold medal. Olympic 10,000-meter run.

A TRAGIC ACCIDENT

At the time Mills envisioned gold, the Australian swimmer Dawn Fraser had already won six medals at the 1956 Melbourne and 1960 Rome Olympics, including two golds in the 100-meter freestyle and another in the 4x100-meter freestyle relay.

She was the queen of the pool, the fastest woman on water, and going into 1964, gunning for gold in the 100-meter freestyle for an unprecedented third straight Olympics.

In fact, Fraser of Balmain, New South Wales in Australia, had set the world record for the 100 meters at the Australian National Championships and Olympic Trials with a time of 58.9 seconds on February 29, 1964, the ninth straight time she had set the world record. She was on top of the swimming world and looking forward to Tokyo seven months later. Fraser's mother, Rose, was in Sydney to watch her daughter break her own record, excited about plans to go to Tokyo and see her, for the first time, compete in the Olympics.

It was past midnight on Sunday, March 8 when the Frasers left a dinner party at the Balmain Rugby League Club. Fraser, who stuck to orange juice that evening, took the wheel of the car so that she could drive her friend, Wendy, her sister, and her mother home. Rounding a curve at forty miles per hour, her headlights revealed a truck parked at the side of the road which suddenly loomed large as Wendy yelled, "Look out!"

Fraser abruptly jerked the wheel to the right, sending the back of the car into the truck and flipping it. Fraser regained consciousness on the grass and noticed blood on her face. She saw Wendy bleeding nearby and then was told that her sister and mother had been transported to a hospital. Fraser passed out and woke up in the hospital in shock, her neck vertebrae chipped. Wendy and Dawn's sister were treated for their injuries. But her mother was dead.

Fraser was under constant sedation. Her room was filled with dozens of flower bouquets. Thousands of letters and cards from well-wishers were sent her way. And yet, the pain—the thought that she was the cause of her own mother's demise—was overwhelming. After all, she was at the wheel.

On top of that, a steel contraption kept her neck and spine in line and immobile, an uncomfortable and unwieldy device that was as much albatross as it was brace. For nine weeks, the neck brace was a constant reminder of her inadequacy as an athlete and as a daughter. The doctors were unclear whether Fraser would ever swim again, and so Fraser had pretty much given up on going to Tokyo.

> But recover she did. And one day in April, she put on a swimsuit, not intending to do anything but dip her feet into the pool. Instead, she slipped into the water, and began a gentle swim. "For maybe twenty minutes, there were just the two of us—the water and me. And it felt good."

As Fraser continued her recovery, she began hearing about the fast times set by up-and-coming American, Sharon Stouder. Once her competitive instincts were aroused, Fraser committed to the hard work of getting back into shape for Tokyo. In the final weeks before leaving for Tokyo, the Australian swim team took off for the northern Australian city of Townsville to train.

Getting back into condition was hard, but getting back into a championship mindset was harder. Fraser credits her teammates:

> My female teammates were absolutely fantastic. I was never left alone. I always had a team member with me. I shared a room with my best friend, Loraine Crapp, and Ruth Everett. When you're a team, you're not alone. I always had milkshakes with my teammates after training, and we'd sit on the beach and talk. That helped me get over the hurt I was going through.

YOU HAVE TWO HOURS TO SHAVE

While Fraser was recovering from her emotional pain in Australia, sixteen-year-old Dick Roth was in America, psyching himself up. Roth's mother was a competitive person, who knew that the mental preparation was as important as the physical training, if not more so.

She would repeat certain phrases to her son over and over, "Always see the race." "See it in your mind." "You know how to do it." And, "Never give up." One of Team USA's swimming coaches, George Haines, was also skilled in understanding what buttons to push to get the best out of his swimmers, each in their own way.

Roth was at the National AAU Men's and Women's Outdoor Championships in Los Altos Hills, California. It was July 31, 1964, the first of a three-day competition, and he had barely qualified for the finals in the individual medley earlier that morning. He was demoralized when he got on the table for a rubdown by Coach Haines. Haines noticed that Roth had not shaved his body. "You have two hours to shave," Haines told him sharply.

Roth woke up from his funk, called his sisters and told them to bring a shaving kit, and made sure his body was smooth. When he set up at lane one, a place befitting a slower speed, Haines decided to push another button.

He walked over, with that clipboard in his hands as he always did, and he looked at me and said, "You want me to scratch you out of the race?" I was surprised and said no. He said, "Then get in there and swim!" That's when I set a world record.

BELIEVE

A couple of months before the Olympics, Billy Mills is training in the United States, and he notes in his diary sometime in August that "I'm in great shape, must believe, believe I can run with the best in the world now, and I can beat them in Tokyo."

Mills believed he could will himself to win if he could imagine it. "The subconscious mind cannot tell the difference between reality or imagination," Mills has said in a video interview.[68] "You focus for four years, dozens of times a day, visualizing, re-living the moment the way you want it to be. And then you win. And for one fleeting moment, you know you're the best in the world."

But the reality is, no one else believed Mills would finish in the top three in the 10,000-meter race, let alone win the gold medal. Mills had never finished a 10k race in less than twenty-nine minutes, a time that all of the favorites had surpassed.

68 "Billy Mills. 10000 Meter Gold Medal," YouTube video. Posted [June 24, 2012].

An American had never won a long-distance footrace, and Mills wasn't even the fastest person on the team. His roommate in Tokyo, Washington State University's Gerry Lindgren, had actually won the US trials in the 10k, and was believed by the press to give the United States the best chance. The press wrote hardly a word about Billy Mills.

Then Lindgren hurt his ankle on a training run through Yoyogi Park near the Olympic Village days before the 10,000-meter event. Lindgren would gamely train on, but the favorites for the 10k were now world record holder Ron Clarke of Australia, Mohammed Gammoudi of Tunisia, and Mamo Wolde of Ethiopia. Mills was not even an afterthought.

But Billy Mills was convinced he would take home the gold. He saw firsthand what shape his roommate was in. For his part, Lindgren noted in a later interview that Mills actually took heart from his injury. In fact, on October 12, two days before the race, Mills was exuberant.

> Billy came into our room when I was lying down with the ice pack on my ankle and said, 'Gerry, I can win the gold medal! I can win the gold medal!' His eyes were so wide with excitement. For a day and a half I listened to this as he said he knew he could beat everybody but me and now that I was injured he could win.[69]

69 Gary Cohen, "Interview of Gerry Lindgren," *Gary Cohen Running,* February 2012; garycohenrunning.com.

Lindgren took no umbrage at Mills's self-centered ebullience. "After all," he said, "we were good friends and have always been good friends."

AN EXPLODING APPENDIX? NOT GOING TO STOP ME

"I can withstand pain. In fact, I love pain."

Dick Roth, referred to pain as his "advantage." The high school swimmer who excelled in the 400-meter individual medley believed he could tolerate more pain than almost any of his competitors. And when you're a world-class swimmer, a combination of holding your breath and stretching your body to its physical limits creates severe oxygen debt.

Oxygen is vital to breaking down glucose, which provides your body with energy. But when the body can't get enough oxygen to create energy, it releases lactic acid, a substance that can create energy without oxygen. When there is more lactic acid in your blood than can be burned off, you get pain. And the more intense your physical activity, the more intense the pain will be.

Roth, the world record holder, was one of the young Americans expected to do well. But literally hours after the Opening Ceremonies of the Tokyo Summer Games on October 10, Roth was in pain of another kind. Having gone to bed at 9 p.m., Roth could not fall asleep, a dull ache in his stomach growing in intensity. Tossing and turning, he got out of bed to throw up, and then went to his swim coach, who gave him some medicine. Roth dozed for a while. But at 6 a.m., he woke up to piercing pain, and went straight to the Olympic Village infirmary.

The nurse poked and probed. The swim team doctor did blood tests. And then he was left alone to his thoughts in bed, only twenty-four hours from competing in the Olympic Games. "This is not the way to calm me down," thought Roth. Then came the shock: he was told he had to have his appendix removed, as soon as possible. And he had to be transported to a US Army Hospital in far-off Western Tokyo, immediately.

> "I was so blown away they had to bring in a counselor to calm me down," Roth wrote on his Facebook page in commemoration of his achievement fifty years later. "The ambulance ride to Tachikawa was a blur. The only thing I remember is pulling up to the hospital entrance and thinking I was going to die."

The doctors told Roth that they would take out his appendix right away. Roth, to the surprise of the medical staff, refused surgery. The Army hospital officials asked a member of the US Olympic Committee to sign off on the operation since Roth was still a minor at seventeen, but the USOC felt that it wasn't their decision to make. Instead, they tracked down Roth's parents who were in Tokyo sightseeing at the time. And Roth's parents, of course, were ready to approve the operation. But their son was adamant.

> My parents came in to see me before they signed, thank god. I begged them not to let the doctors take it out. I really wanted to swim. What if they were wrong? So began hours of debate back and forth with phone calls to the States to doctors for third and fourth opinions. In the end, my parents made a deal to take all responsibility, an unbelievably tough decision.[70]

The Roths and the doctors agreed that their son would not exercise except to swim in the heats and that he would have blood tests every four hours. Roth was back in the Olympic Village that evening and went to sleep. The next day, on October 12, he swam relatively poorly in the heats, fifteen seconds slower than his personal best, but still made it into the finals.

THREE TIMES GOLDEN

A day later, on October 13, at 8 p.m., Dawn Fraser lined up with seven other swimmers for the 100-meter freestyle finals. This group included Sharon Stouder and Kathy

---

70 Dick Roth, from his personal posts on Facebook.

Ellis of mighty Team USA, which ended up taking twenty-nine of the total fifty-six swimming medals up for grabs.

Prior to the race, in the massage room, Fraser made a public display of confidence, facetiously faking aches and pains while getting rubbed down. But the truth was, the pressure on Fraser was immense, as she noted in her autobiography, *Dawn: One Hell of a Ride*:

> If any of those competitors had been able to see inside my head or my heart they would have been able to get an edge. No doubt about it. I was frightened. I wanted to vomit and run to the toilet. It was just the most crushing pressure. This race was so important to me and I felt an immense desire to win it for Mum.[71]

When the starter's pistol fired, Fraser jumped out to a lead. She later claimed that she started off too "easily," and should have blasted out to a faster sprint. Stouder pressed hard from the start, and Fraser could see her on her right. But the truth is, Fraser led from start to finish, even pulling away at the end to set an Olympic record at 59.5 seconds, and became the first swimmer ever to win gold in the same race three Olympics in a row. It was only seven months earlier she had lost her mother and doubted whether she would even swim again.

---

71   Dawn Fraser *Dawn: One Hell of a Life* (Hodder, 2001), 189.

As I marched out to the dais for the victory ceremony, the crowd gave me a wonderful ovation. I mounted the number one stand, and I just couldn't have felt prouder. I was the first Australian to win a gold medal (in Tokyo) and the only swimmer ever to win three in a row. The tears were just too hard to hold back, so I stopped trying.[72]

TOO MUCH SPEED

They were in their seventies when they met again in London at the 2012 Olympics—old friends, old rivals, Mohammed Gammoudi from Tunisia and Billy Mills of the United States.

Prior to the Tokyo Olympics the two had faced off in a 10,000-meter race in Belgium, which Gammoudi won. In Tokyo, Gammoudi asked Mills if he remembered the advice he gave him in Belgium after the race—"more speed." In other words, he needed to "maintain a faster pace, while still being able to sprint at the end. I would practice running as fast as I could go without losing composure."

When Mills and Gammoudi saw each other in Tokyo in October 1964, they embraced as old friends even though they had met only three times. Mills said they respected

---

72   Dawn Fraser and Harry Gordon, *Below the Surface: The Confessions of an Olympic Champion* (New York: William Morrow & Company, 1965), 226-227.

each other and hoped that both of them would ultimately celebrate on the victory stand. But Ron Clarke, their biggest rival in this competition, and the 10,000-meter world record holder, had similar designs of his own.

At that time, Clarke was world famous, and expected to win. Nobody knew who Billy Mills was.

But with only two laps to go, Mills was still on Ron Clarke's shoulder. Hypoglycemic, blood sugar nearly depleted, Mills was tiring. But then, Clarke looked back, and Mills took that as a sign—"My God, he's worried! If I could just stay with him, I have a chance. I have a chance."

In the final lap, somehow, the Australian Clarke got boxed in front by a runner who had been lapped, Karuananda (the Sri Lankan whose story was told in chapter five), and Mills to his right. "I have Ron boxed in perfectly," Mills explained, looking back at one of the most dramatic moments of the XVIII Olympiad. "He nudged me a little. I nudged him back. He then put his hand under my elbow and pushed me out. I thought I was going to fall. I went out and stumbled. I closed back on his shoulder. It was then that Gammoudi from Tunisia broke between us."

Gammoudi told Mills all those years later in London that he thought Mills was done—"My friend is off balance, and out of the race, but I must focus on Ron, the world record holder." Gammoudi told Mills he believed it was his moment to strike, when he elbowed his way through Clarke and Mills.

Mills said that coming around the final bend, in his low blood-sugar state, he could hear nothing but the throbbing of his heart and feel nothing but a tingling sensation along his forearm, his vision coming and going, but he somehow pushed himself to give it "one more try."

So with eighty yards to go, Mills visualized victory, telling himself, "One more try, one more try." And then, "I can win, I can win, I can win." And finally, "I won, I won, I won, I won." And yet Mills was still in third place. Sprinting in the middle lanes, using precious energy to swing outside but also taking advantage of firmer ground on the rain-soaked cinder tracks, Mills lifted his legs and pumped his arms in an amazing burst, the incredible finish described in gleeful shrieks by the American announcer for NBC, Dick Bank: "Look at Mills! Look at Mills! Coming on! Mills is coming on! Oooh hoo! What a tremendous accomplishment! Bill Mills wins the 10,000 meters in a tremendous upset!"

Mills crossed the finish line as the first and only American to win the 10,000-meter race. A Japanese official came up to him and said, "Who are you?" Mills was struck with fear, thinking he had not run enough laps to complete the race. Reassured that he had indeed won, his friend from Tunisia, the second-place finisher, came up to congratulate him.

Gammoudi gave Mills a big smile and said, "Too much speed."

Billy Mills wins gold in the 10,000 meters, courtesy of Marine Corps Photo # A411758 [Public domain]

INSPIRED TO A WORLD RECORD VICTORY

On October 14, Roth was getting himself mentally ready for the 400-meter individual medley. The pain of his appendicitis had been managed. But he had a long wait as his event wasn't until the evening. Killing time, Roth listened to the Olympics coverage on his new transistor radio. He caught the end of the 10,000-meter race, listening to the last three laps. Roth was rooting for Gerry Lindgren, who was thought to have the best chance of becoming the first American to win the 10k, but labored with his injured ankle and finished ninth. But then, quite dramatically, Roth learned about the other American in the race.

I don't know what got into him, but Billy Mills gave us one of the greatest Olympic moments ever. He ran by Clarke and Gammoudi like they were out for a nice Sunday jog and won the race by two meters! The dorm erupted in a roar, waking up my roommates. I could barely tell them what had happened I was so excited! I began to say over and over to myself: "If he can do it, I can do it, too. If he can do it, I can do it, too." Trouble was, I had about eight hours until my race.

All he could do was sit with his thoughts on the upcoming medley, the multidisciplinary race that stretches the boundaries of endurance and pain for the very best swimmers in the world.

"Everyone is on the same level physically," Roth said. "So it is all mental. On any given day anyone can win. We all knew about pain. You had to swim through the pain. I would get myself into oxygen debt and when I couldn't add two and three, when I thought I couldn't go any further, I knew I was in the right place."

Pain was a part of his mental preparation. "All that day I swam the race in my mind and felt the pain over and over and over. I was obsessive. But I got to watch my confidence build back up. I remember it very clearly." What Roth didn't remember clearly was the actual 400-meter medley finals race, which consists of 100-meter sprints in four different styles: butterfly, backstroke, breaststroke, and freestyle.

> I really don't remember the race very well. I remember being out of the race in the butterfly, probably back in fifth or sixth place. I do remember turning over for the backstroke because you can breathe. I then remember in the breaststroke taking a couple of breaths, not looking around, but bearing down internally. And I remember the last half lap and the searing pain, complete bodily pain. Oxygen debt. Muscles don't have enough oxygen. The pain of lactic acid. My advantage. I always had something in the tank.

And then some. Roth smashed his own world record by three seconds, a time of four minutes, 45.4 seconds that lasted nearly four more years. The pain of the appendicitis, the searing burn of lactic acid—all that faded away as he stood on the podium to receive his gold medal.

Back home after the Olympics, amidst visits to the White House, dinners, speeches, and TV appearances, Roth did finally have that appendix removed. And what happens to such unique artifacts of Olympic importance? In this case, the appendix of Dick Roth sits in the International Swimming Hall of Fame in Fort Lauderdale, Florida.

CHAPTER 8

WHERE THERE'S A WILL THERE'S A WAY

THE TRIUMPH OF THE JAPANESE WOMEN'S VOLLEYBALL TEAM AND A NATION REBORN

In the open weight judo finals at the 1964 Tokyo Olympics, Japan's best, Akio Kaminaga, lost to the giant Dutchman, Anton Geesink late in the afternoon on Friday, October 23, the penultimate day of the Olympiad. In defeating Kaminaga, Geesink had also sunk Japan's hopes of sweeping gold in the only sport at the Olympics native to Japan.

A few hours later, about thirteen kilometers southwest of the Nippon Budokan, site of Kaminaga's defeat, the

Japanese women's volleyball team was preparing for their finals at the Komazawa Indoor Stadium. They too were going up against bigger, stronger adversaries—the USSR.

Hirobumi Daimatsu, coach of the women's volleyball team, understood the challenge and worked over the years to train his players to compensate for relative weaknesses in size and strength with speed, superlative technique, and guts. Daimatsu, called the "demon" early on by his players, was ferocious in his training methods. The Western press would witness "Demon Daimatsu's" practices, and call it abuse.

And even on the day of the finals on October 23, Daimatsu had his team go through a tough four-hour training session. This was war to Daimatsu. A veteran of battles in China and Burma during the Pacific War, he believed he had to get his team into a battle mindset, as he describes in his book, *Follow Me*:

> Games are like fighting with real swords. Sports today are either kill or be killed. The metaphor of killing may not be proper, but second place means nothing. Unless you are number one...[your efforts] are meaningless.[73]

This time, on the wooden floor of the gymnasium, the

---

73 Yoshikuni Igarashi, *Bodies of Memory: Narratives of War in Postwar Japanese Culture, 1945-1970* (Princeton, NJ: Princeton University Press, 2000), 156.

enemy was the Soviet Union, a nation that had declared war in the final week of the Pacific War.

DEMON DAIMATSU CHANNELS POSTWAR DEMONS

The film, *Nichibou Kaizuka Volleyball Team*, produced in 1963, can still make one cringe over fifty years later.

The male coach repeatedly throws a volleyball to the right and to the left of a young woman whose sole mission is to get a hand on the ball. Lunging desperately, arm extended, the woman does a somersault on the hard court, rolling over her shoulder or across her back and landing on her feet in a single motion, in order to begin running the other way so she can desperately get to the next ball thrown to a different part of the court...back and forth, down and up, over and over again...until she's so tired she does not realize her body is simply moving on its own.

This technique is called "*kaiten reshibu*" (receive and rotate) and was one of the secret weapons that made Japan's women's volleyball team so effective in the Sixties. When they marched into Moscow to take on the mighty Soviet Union in the 1962 world championships, where the Soviet team was not only on its home court, but had a distinct height and strength advantage, the Japanese entered the arena as underdogs. They left it as world champions.

The Soviet press was so amazed by the speed and agility of the Japanese that it dubbed them "The Oriental Witches," a designation that the international press took up with relish. Interestingly, the Japanese press and the team members themselves took to that title with pride.

"In Japan, 'witch' (*majo*) is a scary thing," said team captain, Masae Kasai in an interview with Helen Macnaughtan of SOAS, University of London. "But the nickname wasn't meant to reflect this. It was a word to describe our volleyball play, which had never been seen before: techniques such as 'receive and rotate.'"[74]

Daimatsu knew that the Japanese had to find a way to compensate for their weaknesses. The Japanese women were smaller, so they had to be quicker, more efficient, more willing to sacrifice their bodies. And so his practices were unrelentingly—demonically—hard.

And while the end seemed to justify the means—the women's volleyball team under Daimatsu had never lost—some wondered whether the coach was crossing the line and abusing his players. In a Japanese NHK documentary[75] the labor union of the company that employed the members of the women's volleyball team criticized

---

74 Helen Macnaughtan, "An Interview with Kasai Masae, Captain of the Japanese Women's Volleyball Team at the 1964 Tokyo Olympics," *Japan Forum* (October 12, 2012): 497.

75 NHK, Dokyumento. Supôtsu tairiku, 21 May 2005.

Daimatsu for his training regimen. But "the union's objections did not seem to matter, either to the coach or to management."[76]

Overseas journalists also thought that the women were being abused, as you can tell from the title of a *Sports Illustrated* article, "Driven Beyond Dignity." In this March 16, 1964 piece, the writer, Eric Whitehead, described the punishing practices that Daimatsu put his players through.

> Daimatsu signals, and in rapid rotation the girls charge toward the net, crisscrossing from their respective corners. With the ball girl feeding him swiftly, silently, Daimatsu swings his fist in a swift, rhythmic motion, slamming the balls first to one side and then the other as the girls come charging in. The balls are aimed deliberately short so that the girls must hurl themselves headlong in a desperate, often futile attempt to retrieve and keep them in the air. They land jarringly on their chests and shoulders, then roll out and recover with a sprawling, judo-like somersault.
>
> As each girl recovers, she dashes back to the wall to charge in immediately for the next retrieve, sometimes as many as six times before the next girl comes hurtling in. An hour of this and the girls are sweat-sodden, soiled, and gasping with the exertion. After two hours, Daimatsu, expression-

---

76 Iwona Merklejn, "Remembering the Oriental Witches: Sports, Gender and Showa Nostalgia in the NHK Narratives of the Tokyo Olympics," *Social Science Japan Journal* 16 (June 2013): 246.

less, his arm still swinging like a piston, closes the range. He now imparts a vicious spin to the ball. A heavyset girl lumbers in, overcharges, slams onto her shoulder and grimaces in pain as she hobbles drunkenly back to the wall, where she bends in agony. Daimatsu, his motion unbroken, is now jibing softly, "If you'd rather be home with your mother, then go. We don't want you here."

Another girl hurtles to the floor, goes sprawling across the court and hits an ankle against an iron bench with a sickening crack. She is sobbing as she limps back to the wall. "There's a South Korean team in town. If this is too tough for you, maybe you should go and play with them."[77]

Was this tough love? Was it abuse? In the end, team captain Kasai said that the players had nothing but respect for their coach:

I had a lot of trust and respect for Coach Daimatsu. The team was happy to take direction from him because we trusted him. He was a volleyball player himself when he was a university student. He joined Nichibo after being a soldier in the war. The team and I followed his hard training because of his great human nature. He was a man we could trust and respect as a human being. Whenever our team won, we were convinced that his hard training was the right way to go, and so we would practice and train hard

77   Eric Whitehead, "Driven Beyond Dignity," *Sports Illustrated*, March 16, 1964.

again, and then we would win again. There was a very close bond between him and the team.[78]

Along with the women's volleyball team, Daimatsu was a national hero, whose books on leadership, *Follow Me!* and *Where There's a Will There's a Way*, were bestsellers. In them he writes that his war experience shaped his coaching philosophy.

Daimatsu fought in China and Burma under horrendous conditions, always marching, seemingly always in the hard rains of Southeast Asia, scavenging for bamboo shoots dug up from the dirt to stay alive. Eventually he developed a case of hemorrhoids so painful that he could not walk. Yoshikuni Igarashi, in his book, *Bodies of Memory*, about Japan's postwar years, wrote how Daimatsu's suffering in WWII became lessons for his volleyball team:

> Although at one point he was ready to give up and be carried on a stretcher, he realized that once he stopped walking, he would only grow weaker and die. So, he kept walking, telling himself all the while: "Don't sleep. Don't sleep. You are gonna die once you sleep." Many others did die. He claims that only those with strong willpower sur-

---

78   Helen Macnaughtan "An Interview with Kasai Masae, Captain of the Japanese Women's Volleyball Team at the 1964 Tokyo Olympics," *Japan Forum*, October 12, 2012, 496.

vived. His life philosophy emerged out of his own survival: he could accomplish anything insofar as he willed it. [79]

At the war's end, Daimatsu was taken prisoner and sent to a British POW camp in Rangoon, Burma, where he writes in *Follow Me!* that he and other Japanese prisoners were forced to clean toilets with their bare hands, humiliated for not washing the undergarments of female officers properly, and restrained from helping colleagues who died in front of them. As Igarashi writes, the lesson that Daimatsu took from his POW experience was clear:

> Through his miserable experiences in the POW camp after the defeat of Japan, he learned the reality of war: "winning is everything." As a result of these experiences, volleyball became for Daimatsu not merely a sport but a means of Japan's historical redemption. Daimatsu aspired to make those who had not treated the Japanese as human beings recognize their error by demonstrating the determined spirit of the Japanese to win volleyball games.[80]

JUBILATION

Before the finals with the Soviet women, expectations were running high—not only for the coach who refused

---

79   Yoshikuni Igarashi, *Bodies of Memory: Narratives of War in Postwar Japanese Culture, 1945-1970* (Princeton, NJ: Princeton University Press, 2000), 156.

80   Yoshikuni Igarashi, *Bodies of Memory*, 157.

to let his charges lose, but among the public at large, who understood that this match represented a final chance at the redemption that lay flattened on the judo mat just hours earlier. The pressure on the team was immense. One of the players was quoted in the *Sankei News* a day before the finals as saying, "If we lose, we might have to leave the country."[81]

To say the weight of an entire nation was on the shoulders of these women would be an understatement. To make matters worse, the finals match didn't start on schedule at 7:00 p.m., so the players had to wait around and stew in their tension for an extra thirty minutes.

Watching the women prepare for battle, for those not aware that the Japanese were favorites to win, one might think the odds were stacked against the Japanese.

> Then they entered...twelve strapping Russians in scarlet vests and trunks, pony-tailed hair bobbing, each built like an Amazon, grim, purposeful, determined—and twelve little dark-haired Japanese in white vests and green trunks, who looked like a class of girls following their teachers, crocodile-style, to school. Looking at the comparative

---

81 Sankei News Archive, Osaka no 20 Seki (31), Kaiten Reshiibu 'Tōyō no Majo' Sekai ni Kōfun to Kandō, October 20, 2011.

physique of the teams, it seemed a monstrously unfair contest.[82]

And yet, when the game finally began, the women of Japan simply went about their business, taking the first two sets 15-11 and 15-8.

As Masae Kasai recalled in her autobiography, *Okaasan no Kin Medaru, (Mom's Gold Medal)*, she reminded herself to stay calm, but couldn't help but wonder, "What the heck is wrong with the Soviets?"

In the third set, Japan raced to an 11-3 lead, and at that point Kasai thought, "It's possible, victory is possible." But in the next instant, Kasai got mixed up with a teammate when attempting to receive, and, according to the team captain, the Soviets seemed to catch a second wind. Still, Japan battled on to a 13-6 lead, and then got to match and championship point at 14-8. But momentum switched suddenly to the Soviets, as they fought their way back to within a point to 14-13.

Daimatsu called time out. "What are you doing?" he said. "Calm down. All you need is one point to win, right? Stay loose."[83]

---

82   Doug Gardner, "Into Battle: The Women's Volleyball Team," republished in the book, *The Games of the XVIIIth Olympiad Tokyo 1964* (International Olympic Institute Lausanne, 1965), 267.

83   Masai Kasai, *Okaasan no Kin Medaru, (Mom's Gold Medal)* (Gakken, 1992), 89.

It was Kasai's turn to serve, and she hoped to decide the match then and there, but the Soviets got the serve back. This was a time when you could only win points on your serve, so back and forth it went, both teams failing to capitalize on their own serve five times in a row.

The sixth time was the charm.

Emiko Miyamoto, whipped her super slim left arm through the air, rocketing the ball across the net to the Soviet back court with such velocity that the Soviet receiver's return, which should have been a pass to a teammate in the frontcourt, ended up flying across the net. The Soviet player in the frontcourt saw it heading toward her and hoped to change the ball's direction, but when she tapped it, the ball had already passed over the net. A Japanese player reacted and sent the ball back to the Soviet side, but the referee blew his whistle.

It was 9:01 p.m. and at that moment, the players realized that they had finally reached the peak of a very tall mountain, coming together with jubilant hugs and tears, as a nation erupted in celebration.

Japanese women's volleyball team celebrating gold-medal victory, courtesy of PHOTO KISHIMOTO

They were just factory workers in a textile company, who indeed worked during the day, and practiced during the night and weekends. They were not, as individuals, nearly as tall or as strong as most of their opponents on the other teams. But they had a demanding coach who developed techniques—like "*kaiten reshibu*"—to leverage their speed and team play, who demanded their respect, infused them with confidence, and made them believe that victory was theirs if they wanted it.

They wanted it. They got it. And the nation cheered as it had not in nearly two decades.

At the point of victory that evening, the broadcast of the women's volleyball finals was (and still is) the highest-rated television program ever, sparking a nationwide celebration. It's safe to say that nearly every television set in Japan that was on at that moment was showing the volleyball finals.

For the spectators in the arena as well as the millions watching around the country, the sting of Kaminaga's earlier loss, along with the lingering doubts as to whether Japan, a nation defeated and devastated in war, could organize and present an event worthy of the Olympic tradition—the first ever to be held in Asia—and in the process demonstrate that it was ready to take its place as a member in good standing of the global community, fell away as the ball dropped to the floor for the final point of the match.

On that day, October 23, 1964, Japan was a nation reborn—young, confident, world-beaters.

Following the Olympics, inspiring the youth through sports stories became a media industry in Japan. Rio Otomo was a teenager in the 1960s, and after the Olympics found herself among the many students signing up for the volleyball club in her junior high school.

Otomo, in her article, "Narratives of the Body and the 1964 Tokyo Olympics," wrote that a new genre emerged after the Olympics, known as "*supokon-kei*" (or "*supotsu-konjo-kei*"), which can be translated as "willpower-in-sports-genre." It included two popular TV animated series on women's volleyball—*Attaku Nanba Wan* (Attack No. 1) and *Sain wa V* (The Sign is V).

"These stories featuring attractive young athletes," she wrote, "continued to send young viewers monological messages about the importance of endurance, patience, self-sacrifice, faithfulness, and teamwork."[84]

The women of the volleyball team who became heroes in Japan at the 1964 Tokyo Olympics were ordinary people, part of the *shudan shushoku* (group employment) generation, a mass migration of junior high and high school graduates from the countryside to the factories and businesses in the cities. The textile industry, which was a significant part of Japan's growing export-driven economy, benefited especially from this practice.

As Helen Macnaughton explains in her article, "The Oriental Witches: Women, Volleyball and the 1964 Tokyo Olympics," organizing volleyball teams and games within the factories was management's way of ensuring that the young women in their care were keeping busy during nonworking hours, and physically fit. Over time, management saw that volleyball was a powerful way to engender teamwork, as well as to promote their companies as their

---

84   Rio Otomo, "Narratives, the Body and the 1964 Tokyo Olympics," *Asian Studies Review* 31 (June 2007): 122.

teams succeeded in volleyball tournaments staged with student teams or teams from other textile factories.

The volleyball players at the textile company Nichibo, where most of the Olympic team worked, were certainly not viewed as everyday factory workers. But they did have very full days. The captain, Masae Kasai, had a desk job, working every day until 3 p.m., before departing for volleyball practice, which often continued late into the evening.

Fortunately for Kasai, after a punishing practice, her roommates in the work dorm she shared would often roll out her futon bedding for her and place a hot water bottle inside on those cold nights. They also understood that Kasai and the volleyball team were a symbol of pride for the factory.

Emiko Miyamoto and Masae Kasai, courtesy of PHOTO KISHIMOTO

After the Olympics, they were a symbol of pride for the entire nation.

Japan won. When I saw the players hugging and crying, I felt something in my chest also. This was first time in my life to cry after watching sports.

—YUKIO MISHIMA, FROM AN ARTICLE ENTITLED, "THE GIRLS CRIED, I CRIED TOO."[85]

---

85 Yukio Mishima, "Kanojo Mo Naita, Watashi Mo Naita," Houchi Shimbun, republished in the book, *Tokyo Olympic—Bungakusha ni Yoru Tokyo Gorin Zenkiroku* (Kodansha, 2015), 195.

CHAPTER 9

PASSING THE TORCH–FROM 1964 TO 2020

THE LEGACY OF THE MEN'S GYMNASTICS TEAM OF JAPAN

Gymnastics can be stunning to watch. But when it has to be decided which performance is better than another, it comes down to human eyes. While the International Gymnastics Federation does its best to set out clear descriptions of infractions and standards for excellence, in the end, winners are determined based on the observations and subjective thoughts of the individual judges. And as gymnasts continue to set the bar higher and create routines of greater complexity, the standards for judges also need to be readjusted. That is as true today as it was in decades past.

At the 1964 Tokyo Olympics the battle between gymnasts Boris Shakhlin of the Soviet Union and Yukio Endo of Japan was as tight and tension-filled as any at the Games. Up until then, Shakhlin was considered the best in the world, having won nine Olympic medals in Melbourne and Rome, including four gold medals in 1960. In fact, Shakhlin's total Olympic medal haul of thirteen was the most by any male athlete until 1980.

Shakhlin certainly had an opportunity to continue his championship ways in Tokyo. Except that Endo, and perhaps all of Japan, stood in his way.

Vera Caslavska and Yukio Endo, courtesy of PHOTO KISHIMOTO

On Tuesday, October 20, in the Tokyo Metropolitan Gymnasium, before an expectant home crowd, Endo stepped up to the pommel horse, the final event for the individual all-around competition. American gymnast Makoto Sakamoto witnessed Endo's performance. Although Endo held the lead to that point, Sakamoto knew that the pommel horse is always a challenge, arguably the hardest of the six disciplines. "It's the most difficult event to stay on. There are so many opportunities to fall and slip off. You can hit a slick spot, or you sit down."

Endo needed a score in the nines to assure victory. Pommel horse was not his strength, but based on results to that point, Olympic gold was his for the taking. According to the *Japan Times*, Endo had a considerable lead over Shakhlin and his own teammate, Shuji Tsurumi, before the pommel horse optionals. A solid routine, without significant errors, would win it.

Unfortunately, Endo had what could only be described as a poor effort. As American gymnast Dale McClements described in her diary at the time, "Endo sat on the horse two times and dismounted with bent legs."

"Japanese spectators were biting their nails, fearing that the last-minute errors would cost Endo the gold medal," wrote journalist Keiji Kohyama. "The event was halted ten minutes as Japanese team manager, Takashi Kondo, made a strong appeal to the judges that the faults should not be counted too much in the scoring."[86]

The Japanese pleaded. The Russians glowered. But finally the judges made their decision, and the partisan crowd exploded. The four judges all flashed scores of 9.1, assuring Endo of gold.

Sakamoto, the strongest member of the American men's gymnastics squad, was in disbelief. He missed!

> I remember saying, "Darn it, the best gymnast in the world is crumbling." Then he got a 9.1, and I thought, "What a gift! Anyone else would have gotten an 8.2 or 8.4. He got a 9.1."

Only 0.55 separated Endo from Shakhlin and Tsurumi, who both tied for silver. A score in the low to mid eights would have flipped the order. But the judges saw it the way they saw it and awarded Endo the championship.

Endo's teammate, Shuji Tsurumi, was realistic. Like Shakhlin, his chance for a gold medal rested on the eyes and hearts of the judges and was out of his control. "This is always the way it is," he said.

---

86 Kenji Kohyama, "Endo Causes Scare—2 Gold Medals Won by Japan Gymnasts," *The Japan Times*, October 21, 1964.

Shakhlin also took his defeat in stride. "In my opinion, Endo performed very well, but his side horse play was very poor. However, the international judges were good as a whole. I think I did fairly well as a whole. I can say, now, Endo was the strongest gymnast in the Tokyo competition."

In 1960, the Japanese men's gymnastics team won their first ever team gold at the Rome Olympics. In 1964, they asserted their superiority by winning gold for the second time, sparking a run that would result in five consecutive Olympic championships—a run that covered seventeen years, and could only be described as dominating.

After 1980, however, the teams' Olympic fortunes waxed and waned, and when Japan's gymnasts won the team gold at the 2016 Rio Olympics it broke a drought of twelve years. The undisputed star of that competition was Kohei Uchimura, who also won his second individual all-around Olympic gold. Kohei's parents, both gymnasts themselves, instilled a love for the sport in their son from an early age.

Uchimura's father and mother both worked in Nagasaki for an educational company called Kawai, which had classrooms across the country that offered music lessons, as well as dance and gymnastics. Uchimura's father coached gymnastics, while his mother taught dance at

Kawai. They would eventually form their own gymnastics school together where they trained their son, Kohei, and others to become world-class gymnasts.

And who was it that first hired Mr. and Mrs. Uchimura? None other than Shuji Tsurumi, the four-time medalist from the 1964 men's gymnastics team, who opened up Kawai Gymnastic schools all over the country after this business was established in 1967.

Shuji Tsurumi, courtesy of PHOTO KISHIMOTO

RESTORING THE REPUTATION OF THE DEFEATED ENEMY

In 1964, Japan was preparing an extravaganza for the world, and they just had to get it right. Over 5,000 athletes from over ninety nations were coming to Tokyo. So were thousands of government and sports officials, members of the press, coaches, athlete-family members and sports fans from all parts of the world. If they could show the world that they were peace-loving, Western-like, modern and eager to contribute, then they could stand tall with the other great nations of the world.

Only two decades before, the Japanese were considered Asian upstarts, aggressors, and in some parts, cruel barbarians who would die for the Emperor without a thought. The 1964 Tokyo Olympics was the biggest coming-out party in Asian history, and Japan wanted to change perceptions, and look its absolute best.

Hundreds of known pickpockets were plucked off the streets by police months in advance. Gangs were prevailed upon to send their scarier-looking yakuza out of town. Signs were posted around the city declaring that urinating in the streets or littering would not be tolerated. Bars were closed by midnight. Taxi drivers were advised to drive with "proper traffic manners." Local citizens brushed up on their English and, overcoming their normal reticence, proactively sought out foreign visitors who looked as though they might need guidance. For a while, "May I help you?" was the most commonly heard phrase on the streets.

Stories abounded about the lengths to which the Japanese hosts went to look after visitors in need of help. To rescue an Australian couple who had lost bullet train tickets to Kyoto, their hotel voucher and a notice of remittance so they could pick up cash at a local bank branch, the manager of the Japan Travel Bureau at the pier where they docked raised money from his own staff to buy new train tickets, called the hotel and arranged for the couple to stay without the voucher, and made arrangements with the bank so the cash would be made available.[87]

When a European prince reported his Dunhill tobacco pouch lost at the equestrian event at Karuizawa, an entire Self-Defense Force platoon combed the 33-kilometer course and found the pouch in less than an hour. [88] A journalist who had dropped his signed traveler's checks—in a nightclub as it turned out—got them back after the Mama-san spent two days tracing and deciphering his illegible scrawl, and then rang the hotels and the Press House before finally discovering to whom they belonged.[89]

Billy Mills, hero of the 10,000-meter event, also came in for some of Japan's famous *omotenashi* (hospitality). As a Native-American subjected to his own share of suffering back home, he empathized with his hosts:

---

87 "JTB. Workers Pass Hat for Pocket-Picked Australian," *The Mainichi Daily News*, October 15, 1964.

88 "SDF to the Rescue," *The Japan Times*, October 22, 1964.

89 Christopher Brasher, *A Diary of the XVIIIth Olympiad* (Stanley Paul & Co., 1964), 55.

In Japan, I saw people who were so courteous and polite. I knew underneath there had to be this anger. I could relate to the pain. Almost a sacredness of the way they contained the pain, and the respect they showed. They were like the elders I knew, who controlled their pain, and still showed respect to others.

Mills and his wife, Pat, had plans to return to the United States a day before the end of the games and so would not be joining the USOC-arranged transport to the airport. When the USOC refused to make any special arrangements for Billy—an amateur with little discretionary cash in his pocket—he turned to his Japanese hosts, who expressed surprise that the Americans would not take care of a gold medal winner and one of their biggest stars.

They picked up our bags, and put them in the largest, widest limousine I had ever seen, with Japanese and Olympic flags up front and an American flag on the back. We took off with two motorcycles escorting us to the airport. We left Japan in style.

The XVIII Olympiad was Japan's big test. And if they passed, they thought, the world would welcome them back with open arms. And they did indeed pass that test, thanks to a stunning alignment of purpose across government, corporations, educational institutions, and local neighborhoods. As Azuma Ryūtarō, Tokyo governor and member of both the IOC and Tokyo Olympics Organizing Committee, wrote in 1965:

> One of the intangible legacies of the Tokyo Olympics is that it gave Japanese people the opportunity to be united for the first time since World War II. Additionally, the Tokyo Olympics succeeded in playing a vital role in connecting the East and West in terms of worldwide peace and sports. As a result, the world began to show greater respect for Japan and its people.[90]

BUILDING A REPUTATION OF PEACE AND FRIENDSHIP

The 1964 Tokyo Games were the first Olympics to be held in Asia, and if Japan was bursting with pride, so, too, were many of its Asian neighbors. Thus it was decided that the tradition of transporting the Olympic flame to the host country should include a roadshow through the world's largest continent.

From August 21 to September 6 the torch wended its way through Eurasia, first from Greece to Istanbul. After a day in Turkey, the flame hopped on a plane to Beirut, Lebanon, and then to Teheran, Iran. The course continued to Lahore, Pakistan; New Delhi, India; Rangoon, Burma;

---

90 Satoshi Shimizu, "Rebuilding the Japanese Nation at the 1964 Tokyo Olympics: The Torch Relay in Okinawa and Tokyo," from *The Olympics in East Asia: Nationalism, Regionalism, and Globalism on the Center Stage of World Sports* (Yale University, CEAS Occasional Publication Series, Council on East Asian Studies, 2011), 44.

Bangkok, Thailand; Kuala Lumpur, Malaysia; and Manila in the Philippines.

The crowds in many of these locations reflected the excitement of Asia's first Olympics. The torch bearers were local citizens, and they bore the symbol of the red rising sun on their white tank top jersey, a symbol that in some parts of Asia evoked hatred only two decades prior. Through the 16,000 kilometers that the sacred flame traveled before arriving in Tokyo, Japan's brand in Asia benefited from its association with the Olympic rings and the sacred torch, symbols of peace.

For Robbie Brightwell, the UK athletics team captain, the 1964 Tokyo Olympics was a watershed moment in Olympic history. Brightwell, who helped his 4x400-relay team to a come-from-behind silver medal running the anchor leg in the finals, said that Tokyo "internationalized the Games."

> Up to Rome, 1960, the Olympics was perceived primarily as a mash between European and North American competitors. Tokyo internationalized the games. It was a historical moment for Asia, and I had the feeling that the Olympic ring that represented Asia was finally added for real.

> It was Tokyo that took the Olympic torch to Asia. The torch was a tremendous promotional vehicle. You didn't need a

celebrity. You needed a torch. It could be carried by anyone, and it awakened people all over Asia of the forthcoming Tokyo Olympics.

"We were all conscious that it was the first Asian Olympics," said the captain of the gold-medal winning field hockey team from India, Charanjit Singh. "And during that period the Japanese just rose to the occasion. There was so much devastation (after the war). But instead of giving up, they built it back up themselves. The Olympics were a very good show there, and it showed the world that Asian people can do it very well, like the rest of the world."

THE FIRST EVER OLYMPIC WEDDING

For all of us who fly, it's a sinking feeling when you arrive in a foreign land and your luggage hasn't arrived with you. Imagine if you're an Olympic athlete, and you land without your official uniform, training gear, and other personal belongings. "I was numb with distress," said Diana Yorgova, a long jumper from Bulgaria. Fortunately, among the Japanese welcoming the Olympians at Haneda Airport were two legendary athletes, Mikio Oda, Japan's first-ever gold medalist, who won the triple jump competition at the 1928 Amsterdam Olympics, and Chuhei Nambu, who also took gold in the triple jump at the 1932 Los Angeles Olympics.

Nambu came up to Yorgova to comfort her, and told her

that it would be OK, that in fact, he, too, had landed in Los Angeles without his luggage, and had made his first jump barefoot! She understood. But she was still unsettled. That feeling disappeared the next day.

> After a sleepless night of worry and jet lag, the new day offered me a pleasant surprise: a huge parcel addressed to me containing a brand-new outfit, absolutely my size from spikes and runners to training suit and, moreover, amazingly, a T-shirt with the national state emblem embroidered on it. I was stunned, deeply touched and full of admiration. I wanted to fly with joy because I knew now I was going to participate! In my thoughts I sent thousands of thanks to those Japanese who brought back my self-confidence and dignity and whom I not only didn't even know but had unwittingly disturbed.

Yorgova would place a respectable sixth in the women's long jump competition, her medal to come later with a second-place finish at the 1972 Munich Games. To celebrate her strong performance in her first Olympics, Yorgova and her fiancé, Bulgarian gymnast Nikola Prodanov, decided to do some very special shopping: wedding rings. They planned to hold their big day after their graduation from Sofia University on Prodanov's birthday in May of 1965.

That same day, the couple went to visit the Bulgarian

ambassador, Christo Zdravchev. When the ambassador saw the rings, he brought out a bottle of Bulgarian wine and toasted to the couple's happy future. But then, despite the diplomatic nature of the ambassador's job, he apparently let the cat out of the bag by informing members of the Tokyo Olympic Organizing Committee, who in turn implored the ambassador to request Prodanov and Yorgova to change their plans. Wouldn't it be wonderful, they enthused, for the young Bulgarian couple to hold their wedding in Japan, in the Olympic Village, during the Olympic Games?

The next day, the ambassador sheepishly approached Prodanov and Yorgova with the surprising request.

"Thus our fairy tale began," said Yorgova. "I can't forget the attention and care with which the Japanese ladies of the beauty parlor in the Olympic Village were preparing me for the ceremony. There, for the first time in my life, I had my hair dressed and my nails polished by professionals, who also massaged my scalp and even my arms. When I saw and put on the most beautiful dress of white lace and Nikola put on the first tuxedo in his life, we felt like the prince and princess of a fairy tale."

It was October 23rd, 1964, the day before the closing ceremony. Prodanov and Yorgova were nervous and filled with mixed feelings as this impromptu wedding meant that instead of sharing the moment with families and friends in Bulgaria, they were sharing it with diplomats, administrators, and athletes, as well as press from around the world.

With the civil ceremony completed at the Bulgarian Embassy, the couple then embarked on what can only be described as a most original wedding: Western Olympic Shinto.

Japanese who choose a traditional wedding take their vows before a Shinto priest. But this was something more than just a traditional wedding. Held at the Yoyogi Olympic Village International Club, Prodanov in a black morning coat and Yorgova dressed in a white lace gown and veil entered in the glare of television lights and hundreds of flashing cameras, as they came to take their places in front of the presiding priest.

The traditional Shinto arrangements of sake bottles and rice, along with photos of the Olympic cauldron and the ever-present Olympic rings forming their wedding backdrop, were reminders that they were a long way from home in Bulgaria. An interpreter stood by to explain some of the more confusing aspects of the ritual. In Yorgova's words:

We made our oath of allegiance to the Olympic Flag and a

huge poster of the Olympic Flame in the presence of out-standing athletes from all over the world, official guests, and journalists. To a background of gentle Shinto music we exchanged our rings, drank three sips of sake, and cut the most magical cake of our lives. At the end, we all danced Bulgarian traditional dances *horo* and *ruchenitsa*.

Wedding of Nikolai Prodanov and Diana Yorgova, courtesy of PHOTO KISHIMOTO

If one event symbolized the Olympics' singularly inter-national character, this may have been it.

After the ceremony, the couple was whisked away to the brand-new bullet train to enjoy a honeymoon evening in Kyoto and return to Tokyo the next morning to participate in the closing ceremonies in the afternoon.

Fifty-three years later, Yorgova recalled that magical

moment with gratefulness. "As parents and grandparents of four grandchildren, we value the great efforts of the organizers more than ever before, and we apologize most heartedly for the extra anxiety, inconvenience, and problems we caused to organize our wedding on such short notice," she said. "We lived a moment we will never forget, thanks to the kind and gentle people of Japan, so full of goodwill."

BUILDING A REPUTATION OF RESILIENCY AND HOPE

The Japanese economic miracle captured the imagination of the world. Who expected a nation defeated, devastated, impoverished and under the thumb of its conqueror at the end of World War II, to ever make it back as a contributing partner in the community of nations—let alone accomplish the feat in less than two decades?

Hosting the Olympics and welcoming the world to a modern, confident Japan was a source of deep satisfaction to the Japanese. Yoshihiko Morozoni, a vice minister of the Ministry of International Trade and Industry during the 1960s, felt that pride intensely.

> "Everyone wanted to make Japan a leading nation," he said. "We were desperate to rid ourselves of shame and restore national pride after being defeated in the war. That's the feeling we all harbored unconsciously. And the first thing

that came to our minds was that we should make full use of our industrial ability. Why did we think this? Because we were confident of the ability of the Japanese people."[91]

Prime Minister Hayato Ikeda, a fiery leader who predicted in the early 1960s that Japan's GDP would soon surpass those of major Western economies such as Britain and France, had the same idea. Guaranteeing that the diligence and high educational level of Japan's workforce—"the best in the world"—would see a doubling of incomes over the next ten years, he assured his constituents that "Japan won't be a developing country forever."[92]

A leader of one of the Asian economic success stories, Dr. Mahathir bin Mohamad, former prime minister of Malaysia, said that "without Japan and the Japanese success story, there would be no role model for the East Asian nations. East Asians are no longer shackled by an inferiority complex."[93]

Japan's rise was a team effort, with government, corporations, and individuals in alignment on the mission to restore the country to economic and global relevance.

---

91 "NHK. A Portrait of Postwar Japan Part 1: Economic Miracle, Shimomura's Theory," YouTube video. Posted [April 2017].

92 "NHK. A Portrait of Postwar Japan Part 1

93 "NHK. A Portrait of Postwar Japan Part 1

The symbolism of the 1964 Tokyo Olympics touched everyone in Japan—nor was it lost on the visiting athletes.

Ollan Cassel, the 400-meter sprinter who started the first leg on America's gold-medal winning 4x400-meter relay team, was keenly aware of how far Japan had come in nineteen years since the end of the war, as he was a member of the US Army.

> It was strange to think that only twenty years earlier, my country fought a brutal war with Japan on land, sea, and air. The nation was destroyed, suffering devastation from two atomic bombs, which finally forced a total and unconditional surrender to General Douglas MacArthur.

> We would often visit the city of Tokyo, shopping or sightseeing, and could find reminders of the war with bullet or bomb scars on buildings and streets. It was also necessary, though, to understand how fast the Japanese had adapted to a democratic government and totally endorsed the free enterprise economy system. They could produce the best cameras in the world and for half the price of one in the USA. Everyone was purchasing cameras. Japan was showing the world they were ready to join the free world as an equal partner.[94]

The film trilogy, *Always—San-chome no Yuuhi* (Always—

---

94   Ollan Cassell, *Inside the Five Ring Circus* (Ollan Cassell LLC, 2015), 40.

Sunset on Third Street) charts the lives of two families in a tight-knit neighborhood in central Tokyo from 1958 to 1964. The films, which were released in the years from 2005 to 2012, track the economic and social trends of Japan as the nation emerges from a decade of postwar misery and subservience to the United States.

In the last segment of the trilogy, *Always—Sunset on Third Street '64*, one of the main characters, a struggling novelist named Chagawa, is happily watching the opening ceremony of the 1964 Tokyo Olympics on his small black and white television. But his wife convinces him that it would be better and more sociable to watch together with their neighbors, the Suzukis, on that family's big color set. As they walk out into the street, they are startled by the roar of jet engines, and the spectacle appearing above their heads. Chagawa calls to his neighbors to come outside to see.

As the Suzukis come out to join the Chagawas, directly above their heads in the clear blue skies are five jets forming the Olympic rings. The immediate audience for the display was the crowd of 70,000 spectators, officials and athletes at the National Stadium a few kilometers away. But this powerful integration of technology and art pierced the hearts of the tens of millions of Japanese who witnessed the spectacle on television, symbolizing for them, that indeed, the sky's the limit.

Suzuki, who has built his auto repair shop after returning from the war with nothing, chokes up at the realization that he and his family, like so many others in Japan, have overcome so much pain, have sacrificed so much and worked so hard to get to this point.

> This whole area was burned out in the war. There was nothing to eat. And now...look at this. So many buildings have gone up around us. And there, rising up before our eyes: Tokyo Tower, the tallest in the world. And now, finally, it's the Olympics!

He then leads his family and friends in a mighty cheer—a cry without shame, proclaiming that indeed Japan is back!

LOOKING TO 2020

An Olympic legacy is commonly thought of as the tangible benefits of having hosted an Olympiad—the new sporting venues or transportation systems, the organizing know-how and the practical technology. But it is also the intangible benefits—the inspiration of an entire generation who see the very best athletes in the world strive to their utmost. And on occasion, citizens of the host nation get to see their own athletes and teams take their country on a thrilling ride to victory. These moments can jolt children and young adults, sparking them to dream, to believe that "anything is possible, even for me!"

This aspect of that first Tokyo Olympics carries great significance today as Japan gears up for its second hosting of the Games in 2020. Once again, the country is seeking to create a symbol of resilience, hope, and forward-looking energy as it faces a future encumbered by events of the recent past.

After the collapse of the financial bubble in the early nineties, the Japanese economy fell into protracted doldrums, a period which came to be known as the "Lost Decades." Markets and corporate profits (with some notable exceptions) languished. Japan was superseded by China as the world's second largest GDP. Overall, Japan's presence on the world stage seemed to have dimmed.

In addition to economic and demographic issues (declining birthrate, rapid aging, the emptying out of rural areas), Japan has been beset by a series of natural disasters: torrential rains, floods, and mudslides that have claimed hundreds of lives and demolished whole communities in the western part of the country; the major earthquake in Kumamoto, Kyushu, in 2016; and most devastating of all, the earthquake and tsunami that struck northeastern Japan and triggered a nuclear disaster, on March 11, 2011. Recovery from that disaster, complicated by radioactive debris and contamination, is still far from complete.

Understanding the power of context, the Tokyo 2020

Bid Committee was wise to select a relatively unknown Paralympian named Mami Sato from the March 11 disaster area to kick off their presentation to the International Olympic Committee in Buenos Aires, Argentina, in 2013. Sato, a two-time Paralympian long jumper, thirty-one at the time, spent long hours of preparation on the speech she had to make in English, a task for which she had almost no background. But her honest and unaffected delivery of a very moving story created an emotional swell of support that helped propel Japan to the winning bid.

> I was nineteen when my life changed. I was a runner. I was a swimmer. I was even a cheerleader. Then, just weeks after I first felt pains in my ankle, I lost my leg to cancer. Of course, it was hard. I was in despair. Until I returned to university and took up athletics.

For Sato, the simple idea in sports of having a goal and working to reach and surpass it became a passion, the loss of her leg serving as a catalyst to a sporting life as a long jumper. Sato competed at the Paralympics in Athens in 2004 and Beijing in 2008.

"I felt privileged to have been touched by the power of sport," she said. "And I was looking forward to London 2012."

Then disaster struck.

The tsunami hit my hometown. For six days I did not know if my family were still alive. And, when I did find them, my personal happiness was nothing compared to the sadness of the nation.

Like so many other survivors of the earthquake and tsunami in Northern Japan, Mami Sato helped others—forwarding messages, talking to victims, delivering food, and even organizing sporting events to take children's minds off the daily worries of the aftermath.

Only then did I see the true power of sport...to create new dreams and smiles. To give hope. To bring people together.

Mami Sato has spent her recent years passing on that power to others—among them a young woman named Saki Takakuwa from Saitama. When Saki was in sixth grade, she loved playing tennis and running in track. One day she felt pain in her left leg after practicing hurdles, a pain that would not go away. It turned out to be a tumor below her knee, and at first the doctor couldn't tell if it was malignant or benign. But after enduring four surgeries, including amputation, chemotherapy, hair loss, and the constant reliance on others for assistance, Takakuwa was despondent, wondering if she would ever walk again.

Her mother, Yoko, was determined to help her daughter turn her mindset around. She received a book from a friend called *Lucky Girl*, by Mami Sato. The mother scanned the book, looking for similarities in experience and stories that might make her daughter feel hopeful for the future. Those stories worked.

> It was inspiring to read such a positive story by someone who'd gone through something similar to me. Her book made me realize there were opportunities out there and that I didn't necessarily have to give up on sport. At a real dark time in my life, it gave me encouragement, but that doesn't mean I suddenly decided to become a Paralympian. At that point I wasn't really thinking about my future at all. It was just about getting through each day.[95]

Even better, a doctor gave mother and daughter a sense of hope they simply had not imagined.

> Once [Saki] becomes accustomed to the prosthetic, she will be able to go to school again. She will be able to go to senior high school and university. She will also be able to find a job and get married.[96]

Buoyed by Sato's example and the doctor's new prognosis, Saki discovered that with practice, she could get around on her prosthetic leg. She could indeed walk again. And

---

95 Matthew Hernon, "Paralympian Saki Takakuwa Is Making Great Leaps," *Tokyo Weekender*, September 2, 2016.

96 Toshihiro Yamanaka, "Paving the Way with a Prosthetic," *The Asahi Shimbun*.

then she learned something even more powerful. By focusing on her thigh muscles and using them to maintain balance, Saki found she could run again, run straight, run hard.

> At that time, I did not know what my own limitations were. But I was just happy to be able to do the same thing as everyone else, so I tried various challenges. I gave it my all in everything I did. I want to continue running while never forgetting that feeling.

Inspired, Takakuwa went on to compete in both the 2012 London Paralympics and the 2016 Rio Paralympics. At the age of twenty-eight, 2020 in Tokyo should be in her sights, with hopes of inspiring others.

Speaking of her own devastated hometown area, Mami Sato told the IOC delegates in Buenos Aires that athletes and their expression of Olympic values, can inspire:

> More than 200 athletes, Japanese and international, making almost 1,000 visits to the affected area are inspiring more than 50,000 children. What we have seen is the impact of the Olympic values as never before in Japan. And what the country has witnessed is that those precious values, excellence, friendship, and respect, can be so much more than just words.

The legacy of the Olympics is the children and young men and women bearing witness to feats of peak performance, honest humility, exhaustive effort, and a perseverance beyond belief. It is also the respect the athletes have for one another, an appreciation on the part of all concerned of cultural differences and strengths, and a chance for the host country to display resilience, competence, goodwill, and hospitality to the rest of the world. Tokyo took full advantage of this opportunity in 1964. By all indications, it appears determined to surpass that performance in 2020.

* * *

American gymnast Makoto Sakamoto was seventeen when he arrived in Tokyo for the Olympics, ready to compete in the National Gymnasium, only two kilometers from where he was born. And his memories of childhood came flooding back. When he was eight and he announced to his classmates at Karasumori Elementary School that he was moving to America, the school bully picked a fight with him. And the bigger boy was just too much for little Makoto. So when the seventeen-year-old returned to Japan, the little boy inside was looking for the bully to give him hell.

But the boy inside also remembered the hope and beauty of the time.

Despite the rubble, and the hunger and the despair around him in those difficult years after the war, little Makoto was happy. His mother, like so many mothers in Japan who were enduring the unendurable, had hope.

"I remember walking down a cobblestone road, going to the public bath with my mother," Sakamoto reminisced. "My mom would look up and say, 'there are a lot of stars tonight. It will be a beautiful day tomorrow.'"

EPILOGUE

THE BALLAD OF THEO AND REIKO

In 1964, Reiko Kuramitsu was a freshman at Ferris College in Yokohama majoring in English, and was recruited to be a guide and translator for the Silk Center, which opened in Yokohama in 1959 to promote the silk industry.

Reiko worked 9 to 5 and was given special permission to skip classes so she could do her civic duty and help foreigners visiting the Silk Center learn about the great industriousness and skill of Japanese craftsmen. Born in Tokuyama-shi (now Shunan-shi), Yamaguchi, in the Western part of Japan, Reiko had progressive parents who encouraged their daughter to study English and expand her horizons.

And with the arrival of the Olympics, Reiko was excited.

> It is hard to believe that it was only nineteen years after the war. It was amazing to make such a quick recovery. All the spirit came back. The whole country was so excited about the Olympics and Tokyo. Most of the people were able to buy TVs, black and white. All of Japan was talking about the Olympics!

And Reiko felt that something special was coming for her. "Before the games started, I had a premonition that something was going to really happen to change my life," she said. "I sensed things were going to happen in the future. I felt it very strongly."

As the Tokyo Olympics were coming to a close, a group of Olympians entered the Silk Center. One of them, an Australian, looked so much like the American actor Steve McQueen, that the workers at the Silk Center were star struck, asking him for autographs. Reiko wasn't interested and walked away from the gaggle of girls. Ted (Theo) Mittet, a young American rower whose story was recounted in chapters three and five, was accompanying faux McQueen, and noticed Reiko. He left the Silk Center without saying a word to her.

But Theo returned the next day. Reiko wasn't there, but her friend, Sumiko, also from Reiko's hometown, was.

Theo asked Sumiko for Reiko's name and where he could contact her. "The next thing I knew, I got this express letter from the Olympic Village from Theo," she said. "It just said, 'Dear Reiko, would it be possible to have dinner together?' He didn't even know me. This must be fate."

They met for dinner in Chinatown—Douhatsu—one of the popular restaurants in Yokohama at the time. Reiko brought her friend, Sumiko, along; after all, she had never met this man before. Reiko sensed that Theo was unhappy that a party of two suddenly became a party of three. And she felt he was annoyed that she didn't know anything about his hometown of Seattle. But she liked him.

> He was cute. He had beautiful brown eyes. More interestingly to me, I learned he was studying to be an architect. I almost went to art school, but instead ended up studying English literature. To me, his interest in architecture meant he was artistic, and that interested me about him more than anything.

They met one more time before Theo took off on his two-month journey through Japan. He even stopped by Tokuyama and met Reiko's mother. After Theo returned to Yokohama, they met several times, but their relationship seemed to stall. And then one day, Theo was gone. He had embarked on a ship that took him around the world before returning home to Seattle.

Still they stayed in touch as pen pals, "just good friends." But as her parents did, Theo encouraged Reiko to be more curious, to be more independent. And at some point, she decided that she would go to the United States, "to see America with my own eyes."

While it is routine for single Japanese women to travel abroad today, in the 1960s, very few Japanese did. Overseas travel was not encouraged by the Japanese government, as they wanted to keep their hard-earned export dollars for use by Japanese corporations. And to get a visa to America, you had to go through a few hoops. She had to have sponsors in America, so she talked with her college teachers, and fellow churchgoers and got introductions to their friends in America. At the church she attended, she knew a Naval Commander named George Imboden, whose daughter she had become friends with.

Thanks to all these connections, she was able to convince the American Embassy she had a clear travel plan and people to meet her along the way. She boarded a ship that took twelve days, passing through the Aleutian Islands before arriving in San Francisco. Then she started her American journey in earnest, pulling out her Greyhound Bus ticket, taking advantage of an unlimited travel promotion called "99 days for 99 dollars."

She was twenty-one. She was on a bus. And she was

seeing America: Colorado; Kansas; Tennessee; Georgia; New York; Massachusetts; Washington, D. C.; Illinois; Iowa. And then back to the West Coast with a visit to Seattle, Washington.

Reiko was met by Theo's family at the Eighth Avenue bus terminal and was shocked to see these big Americans. Like Theo, his father and his brother were both over six feet tall. Reiko met Theo's mother, and her sister. But Theo wasn't there. He was in California, studying at UC Berkley.

So, Reiko made her way south to California. She was able to stay with Commander Imboden at their home in Long Beach. When Theo took a summer job at a nursery in Laguna Beach, he arranged for a homestay for Reiko near him. And they got to know each other for another two months.

With her visa at her limit of six months, Reiko had to head back to Japan. But before she left, Theo and Reiko got engaged. A year later, they married.

If Reiko stayed in Japan, she likely would have ended up in an arranged marriage, and probably would still be in Yamaguchi.

My life is so much richer (for meeting Theo). I can't imagine what would have happened if I had stayed in Japan my whole life.

The year 1964 revealed a new Japan to the eyes of skeptical nations; a world big and diverse to the eyes of the Japanese. With feelings of endless possibility, it was encouraging after all had seemed lost only nineteen years before. It was the greatest year in the history of Japan.

ACKNOWLEDGMENTS

I love to write. I love sports. It must be in my blood.

My father, Thomas, was a print and broadcast journalist, who was present at the 1964 Tokyo Olympics. My mother, Sayoko, was born to a man who ran a local newspaper in Tochigi, and whose brother owned a sporting goods shop called Ryomo Sports, very close to Tochigi Station.

Since the time I decided to write a book on the 1964 Tokyo Olympics, I was on the equivalent of a four-year runner's high. I am grateful for my parents for setting me up for this unique moment and opportunity.

So much of my joy comes from talking to Olympians. I interviewed over seventy, and I've listed all of the 1964 Olympians I interviewed at the end of this section. To each and every one of them, I am grateful for their time and their eagerness to share their memories and insights from those days in Tokyo in 1964.

I want to thank a few Olympians in particular who took extra time to share their stories, as well as connect me to other Olympians: Ron Barak, John Boulter, Kunalan Canagasabai, Ollan Cassell, Ada Kok, Billy Mills, Theo Mittet, Frank Gorman, Abie Grossfeld, Paul Maruyama, Yojiro Uetake Obata, Mel Pender, Makoto Sakamoto, Bob Schul, Jerry Shipp, Andras Toro, Shuji Tsurumi, and Victor Warren.

I have been blessed to work with four young researchers. Three graduates of Waseda University: Rika Suzuki, Shiina Ishige, and Marija Lin translated and summarized Japanese documents for me that helped support my facts and storylines, particularly regarding Kokichi Tsuburaya, and the Japanese women's volleyball team. Rio Royanto uncovered for me tremendous insight into the Indonesian state of mind before they decided to boycott the Tokyo Games.

I am also grateful to Reiko Mittet, who shared her stories of exploration in America; Norio Muroi, who helped me navigate the archives of Pacific Stars & Stripes; Eric Obershaw who provided helpful pointers on conducting research in Japan; Morihiro Numajiri and Megumi Kamiyama of The Seiko Museum for their insight into Seiko's technology at the Tokyo Olympics; and my friend, Kevin Ing, for his advice and ideas in the marketing of my book.

Dr. Helen Macnaughtan and Dr. Martyn Smith of SOAS University of London, as well as Dr. Rio Otomo of the Japan Institute of the Moving Image were all helpful in sharing their insight into the 1964 Olympics, as well as referring me to some great reference materials.

I'd also like to express my gratefulness to authors Julie Checkoway, David Wallechinsky, and Bob Whiting for reading my manuscript and providing feedback. Bob also introduced me to his editor, David Shapiro, whose Occam's razor helped me shape a more concise and flowing narrative.

I also want to thank my friends in the G4—Tom Pedersen, Scott Prina, and Dr. Bob Tobin—for reading early versions of my book and providing feedback and encouragement.

And of course, thank you Noriko, my wife of nearly thirty years, for your love and support. You are my gold medal.

1964 TOKYO OLYMPIANS INTERVIEWED

NAME	SPORT
Auble, Dave	Wrestling
Barak, Ron	Gymnastics
Barry, Bill	Rowing
Boston, Ralph	Long Jump
Boulter, John	Track 800 meters
Bregman, James	Judo
Brightwell, Robbie	Track 400 meters
Campbell, Ben Nighthorse	Judo
Canagasabai, Kunalan	Track 400 meters
Cardin, Marny	Swimming

NAME	SPORT
Caruthers, Ed	High Jump
Cassell, Ollan	Track 400 meters
Cole, Kenneth	Basketball
Collier, Jeanne	Diving
Counts, Mel	Basketball
de Varona, Donna	Swimming
Dillon, Sarinder	Field Hockey
Durbrow, Philip	Rowing
Farrell, Tom	Track 5,000 meters
Fraser, Dawn	Swimming
Gerrard, David	Swimming
Gompf, Tom	Diving
Gorman, Frank	Diving
Grossfeld, Abie	Gymnastics
Grossfeld, Muriel	Gymnastics
Hamid, Supaat	Cycling
Hanni, Eric	Judo
Hansen, Fred	Pole Vault
Hanson-Boylen, Christilot	Equestrian
Haque, Anwarul	Field Hockey
Haslov, Bjorn	Rowing
Heatley, Basil	Track Marathon
Hungerford, George	Rowing
Jackson, Luke	Basketball
Jackson, Roger	Rowing

NAME	SPORT
Jegathesan, M.	Track 200 meters
Jones Smoke, Marcia	Canoeing
Jones, Hayes	Track 110-meter hurdles
Kok, Ada	Swimming
Lassen, Carl Christian	Sailing
Lyon, Dick	Rowing
Maruyama, Paul	Judo
Matsumoto, Fujiya	Sailing
McBryde, John	Field Hockey
McClements Kephart, Dale	Gymnastics
Melges, Harry Buddy	Sailing
Mills, Billy	Track 10,000 meters and marathon
Mitchell, Rusty	Gymnastics
Mittet, Theo	Rowing
Mullins, Jeff	Basketball
Packer, Ann	Track 400 and 800 meters
Pender, Mel	Track 100 meters
Prodanov, Nikolai	Gymnastics
Rahman, Kader	Field Hockey
Roth, Dick	Swimming
Sakamoto, Makoto	Gymnastics
Schul, Bob	Track 5,000 meters
Selvey, Warwick	Discus
Shipp, Jerry	Basketball
Singh, Charanjit	Field Hockey

NAME	SPORT
Singh, Gurbux	Field Hockey
Singh, Harbinder	Field Hockey
Smith Carson, Janell	Track 800 meters
Smoke, Bill	Rowing
Stebbins, Richard	Track 100 meters
Sütő, József	Track Marathon
Svevstrup, Soren	Diving
Tanasugarn, Virachai	Basketball
Toro, Andras	Canoeing
Tsurumi, Shuji	Gymnastics
Tyus, Wyomia	Track 100 meters
Uetake Obata, Yojiro	Wrestling
Warren, Victor	Field Hockey
Webster, Bob	Diving
Williams, Ulis	Track 400 meters
Yorgova, Diana	Long Jump
Zavetchano, Ivan	Judo Coach

ABOUT THE AUTHOR

ROY TOMIZAWA is a leadership and talent development consultant from New York with over 30-years' experience in Asia, working for such companies as MetLife, Nikko Asset Management, Microsoft, DBS Bank, Morgan Stanley and Mercer Human Resource Consulting. A former print journalist for a local Gannett paper outside Philadelphia, Roy was the lead reporter on a team that was awarded 2nd prize in investigative journalism by the Pennsylvania Newspaper Publishers Association for coverage on a maximum-security prison in Eastern Pennsylvania. He is the author of two books on Thailand: *Working with the Thais* (co-author) and *Start Up and Stay Up in Thailand*. He currently resides and works in Tokyo, Japan.